COUNTDOWN TO COMMON CORE ASSESSMENTS

English Language Arts

Mc
Graw
Hill
Education

Bothell, WA • Chicago, IL • Columbus, OH • New York, NY

www.mheonline.com

Mc
Graw
Hill
Education

Copyright © McGraw-Hill Education

All rights reserved. The contents, or parts thereof, may be reproduced in print form for non-profit educational use with *Countdown to Common Core Assessments: English Language Arts*, provided such reproductions bear copyright notice, but may not be reproduced in any form for any other purpose without the prior written consent of McGraw-Hill Education, including, but not limited to, network storage or transmission, or broadcast for distance learning.

Send all inquiries to:
McGraw-Hill Education
Two Penn Plaza
New York, New York 10121

ISBN: 978-0-02-135104-6
MHID: 0-02-135104-X

Printed in the United States of America.

1 2 3 4 5 6 7 8 9 RHR 18 17 16 15 14 13   A

Table of Contents

Teacher Introduction iv

Performance-Based Tasks

Narrative Writing 1 1

Narrative Writing 2 9

Literary Analysis 1 16

Literary Analysis 2 26

Research Simulation 36

Narrative 1 47

Narrative 2 55

Opinion 1 62

Opinion 2 72

Informational 82

End-of-Year Assessment 91

Answer Keys

Narrative Writing 122

Literary Analysis 124

Research Simulation 126

Narrative 127

Opinion 129

Informational 131

End-of-Year Assessment 132

Scoring Rubrics

Prose Constructed Response Scoring Rubric 134

Narrative Scoring Rubric 135

Opinion Scoring Rubric 136

Informational Scoring Rubric 137

Countdown to Common Core Assessments: English Language Arts

Countdown to Common Core Assessments: English Language Arts is an integral part of a complete assessment program aligned to the Common Core State Standards (CCSS). The advances in assessment featured in the Performance-Based Tasks and End-of-Year Assessment include passages and stimulus texts that reflect the increased text complexity and rigor required by the CCSS. The test items require higher-order thinking skills, emphasize the need for students to support responses with text evidence, and feature writing as the result of research, with prompts requiring student understanding of and engagement with the stimulus texts. In a departure from previous high-stakes assessments, individual items align to multiple standards.

NOTE: These tests are intended to familiarize students with the types of items they may encounter on the Common Core assessments. The test scores will provide you with a general idea of how well students have mastered the various skills; the scores are *not* intended to be used for classroom grading purposes.

Overview of Performance-Based Tasks

The Performance-Based Tasks provide students with scenarios that establish a unified purpose for reading and writing. Two distinct types of performance-based tasks are provided. The first five tasks are similar to the tasks students are likely to encounter in states that participate in the Partnership for Assessment of Readiness for College and Careers (PARCC) consortium. The second five tasks are similar to the tasks students are likely to encounter in states that participate in the Smarter Balanced Assessment Consortium.

All of the performance-based tasks provided in this book are appropriate for use in any state, whether consortia-affiliated or independent. Use these tasks in any combination to increase students' comfort level with and understanding of the range of CCSS assessments they may encounter.

Task and Item Types

All of the performance-based tasks assess student integration of knowledge and skills. Each task assesses multiple standards that address comprehension, research skills, genre writing, and the use of English language conventions. The stimulus texts and questions in each task build toward the goal of the final writing topic. Students write across texts to demonstrate their understanding of key elements underpinning the multiple sources.

Each PARCC-style assessment comprises three distinct tasks—**Narrative Writing, Literary Analysis,** and **Research Simulation.** Selected response items generally have two distinct parts. In Part A, students answer a text-based question; in Part B, they support their answer with evidence from the text. The Narrative Writing task uses a single stimulus passage; the Prose Constructed Response (PCR) asks students to complete or further develop the passage in a manner consistent with the existing story elements. PCR items in the Literary Analysis and Research Simulation tasks ask students to craft written essays in response to a variety of stimulus texts.

Each Smarter Balanced-style assessment consists of one of three distinct tasks—**Narrative, Opinion,** or **Informational.** The tasks employ a range of item types to measure student understanding. Research Questions include both selected-response and constructed-response items that test students' comprehension of the stimulus texts and help them to synthesize the information provided by the texts. Students then are directed to craft a written response to the texts and questions.

Administering and Scoring the Performance-Based Tasks

Administer each performance-based task separately. For planning purposes, use the suggested times given below.

- Allow 40 minutes for the Narrative Writing task, 50 minutes for the Literary Analysis task, and 60 minutes for the Research Simulation task.
- Allow 105 minutes for completion of each Narrative, Opinion, and Informational task. During the first 35 minutes, students will read the stimulus materials and answer the research questions; after a short break, students will use the remaining 70 minutes for planning, writing, and editing their responses.

Scoring the Selected-Response and Research Questions

Each Narrative Writing, Literary Analysis, and Research Simulation selected-response item is worth 2 points.

Score two-part items as follows:

- 2 points if both Part A and Part B are correct
- 1 point if Part A is correct and Part B is incorrect or partially correct
- 0 points if Part A is incorrect, even if Part B is correct

Score one-part items as follows:

- 2 points if correct
- 1 point if partially correct
- 0 points if incorrect

For the Narrative, Opinion, and Informational task Research Questions, selected-response items are worth 1 point and constructed-response items are worth 2 points.

Scoring the Essays

Score the Narrative Writing, Literary Analysis, and Research Simulation PCRs holistically on a 13-point scale. Point values are broken down as follows:

- 2 points for addressing the relevant reading comprehension standards [R]
- 7 points for addressing the relevant writing standards [W]
- 4 points for addressing the relevant language conventions standards [L]

A PCR scoring rubric follows the Answer Keys to help you score the essays.

Score the Narrative, Opinion, and Informational task essays holistically on a 10-point scale. Point values are broken down as follows:

- 4 points for purpose/organization [P/O]
- 4 points for evidence/elaboration [E/E] or development/elaboration [D/E]
- 2 points for English language conventions [C]

Genre-specific scoring rubrics follow the Answer Keys to help you score the essays.

Answer Keys

In addition to the responses to the test items, the Answer Keys identify CCSS correlations. The Narrative, Opinion, and Informational task Answer Keys also identify claims and targets met, Depth of Knowledge (DOK), and level of difficulty. You can copy the Answer Keys and use them to track each student's scores.

Overview of End-of-Year Assessment

The End-of-Year Assessment focuses on reading and vocabulary skills, which are assessed by selected-response items. RI or RL standard 1 is the structural component underlying every comprehension item. Additional grade-level comprehension and vocabulary standards address the identification and use of supporting text evidence.

Administering and Scoring the End-of-Year Assessment

Administer the End-of-Year Assessment in two or three sessions, with a short break between each session. For planning purposes, allow 120 minutes per test, excluding the break periods.

Each of the 26 items is worth 2 points. The Answer Key provides a scoring column to create a 52-point test, with multi-part questions eligible for partial credit. In addition to the responses to the test items, the Answer Key identifies CCSS correlations. You can copy the Answer Key and use it to track each student's scores.

Score two-part items as follows:

- 2 points if both Part A and Part B are correct
- 1 point if Part A is correct and Part B is incorrect or partially correct
- 0 points if Part A is incorrect, even if Part B is correct

Score one-part items as follows:

- 2 points if correct
- 1 point if partially correct
- 0 points if incorrect

NOTE: If you prefer to give all items equal weight, give full credit only for completely correct answers and no credit for partially correct answers.

Narrative Writing 1

Today you will read a passage from a book titled *The Bobbsey Twins.* As you read, pay close attention to the plot of the story. You will then answer questions to prepare to write a narrative story.

Read the passage from *The Bobbsey Twins* and answer the questions that follow.

The Bobbsey Twins is a book about two sets of twins in the same family. The story tells about the adventures of these four children. In this passage, Bert, the oldest boy, decides to take his two younger siblings out to fly a kite.

from *The Bobbsey Twins*
by Laura Lee Hope

1   "There is a good breeze blowing," said Bert. "Let us go and fly it on Roscoe's **common**[1]."

2   "I want to see you fly the kite," said Flossie. "Can I go along?"

3   "Yes, come on," said Bert.

4   Flossie had been playing with the kitten and hated to leave it. So she went down to the common with Snoop in her arms.

5   "Don't let Snoop run away from you," said Bert. "He might not find his way back home."

6   The common was a large one with an old disused barn at one end. Freddie and Bert took the kite to one end and Freddie held it up while Bert prepared to let out the string and "run it up," as he called it.

---

common[1]—the name for an open area of land where people relax and enjoy fun activities

GO ON →

Grade 3 • Performance-Based Tasks

7   Now, as it happened, the eyes of Snoop were fixed on the long tail of the kite, and when it went trailing over the ground Snoop leaped from Flossie's arms and made a dash for it. The kitten's claws caught fast in the tail, and in a moment more the kite went up into the air and Snoop with it.

8   "Oh, my kitten!" called out Freddie. "Snoop has gone up with the kite!"

Name: _____ Date: _____

1 **Part A:** What does the word **fixed** tell about Snoop in paragraph 7?

　Ⓐ The kitten is interested in the kite.
　Ⓑ The kitten is afraid of the kite.
　Ⓒ The kitten will take the kite.
　Ⓓ The kitten will rip the kite.

Part B: What does Snoop do right after his eyes are **fixed** on the kite?

　Ⓐ He plays with Flossie.
　Ⓑ He goes inside the barn.
　Ⓒ He jumps on the kite.
　Ⓓ He finds a new kite.

GO ON →

Grade 3 • **Performance-Based Tasks**

Name: _____ Date: _____

2 **Part A:** What do Freddie and Bert do with the kite?

Ⓐ They bring it into a barn.
Ⓑ They fly it in the sky.
Ⓒ They give it to Snoop.
Ⓓ They ask Flossie to fix it.

Part B: Which phrase from the passage shows how they do this?

Ⓐ "... she went down to the common with Snoop in her arms." (Paragraph 4)

Ⓑ "... was a large one with an old disused barn at one end." (Paragraph 6)

Ⓒ "... Bert prepared to let out the string and 'run it up,' ..." (Paragraph 6)

Ⓓ "... over the ground Snoop leaped from Flossie's arms ..." (Paragraph 7)

GO ON →

4   Grade 3 • **Performance-Based Tasks**

Name: _____ Date: _____

3 **Part A:** Why does Flossie take Snoop with her to the common?

Ⓐ She enjoys being with the kitten.
Ⓑ She wants the kitten to ride on the kite.
Ⓒ She wants to let the kitten run around.
Ⓓ She thinks there will be other kittens there.

Part B: Select **two** events that happen because of Flossie's actions.

Ⓐ The kids go to Roscoe's common.
Ⓑ Snoop sees many kites.
Ⓒ The kids have a new problem.
Ⓓ Snoop wants to go home.
Ⓔ Snoop gets into trouble.
Ⓕ The kids learn a new game.

GO ON →

Grade 3 • **Performance-Based Tasks** 5

Name: _____ Date: _____

4 **Part A:** How does Freddie feel about what happens at the end of the passage?

- Ⓐ He thinks it is silly.
- Ⓑ He thinks it is fun.
- Ⓒ He is confused about it.
- Ⓓ He is upset about it.

Part B: How does the reader know how Freddie feels?

- Ⓐ Freddie brings the kite to the common.
- Ⓑ Freddie walks down to the old barn.
- Ⓒ Freddie wants to fly the kite.
- Ⓓ Freddie calls after the kitten.

GO ON →

Name: _____ Date: _____

5 Look at the picture in the passage. Use the picture to help describe what happens in the passage. Write **one** word in each box in the chart.

Words		
Outside	**Characters**	
Angry		
Children	**Setting**	
School		
Adults	**Mood**	
Worried		

Grade 3 • Performance-Based Tasks

GO ON →

Name: _____ Date: _____

6 In the passage, the author tells about what happens when Bert, Freddie, and Flossie go to Roscoe's common. Think about what happens and how the characters act. The passage ends with Snoop, the kitten being carried up into the sky with the kite.

Write a story that continues where the passage ended. In your story, be sure to use what you have learned about the characters and the setting to tell what happens next.

Use the space below to plan your writing. Write your story on a separate sheet of paper.

STOP

Grade 3 • **Performance-Based Tasks**

Narrative Writing 2

Today you will read an article about a special kind of ant titled "Leafcutter Ants." As you read the text, you will gather information and answer questions about these ants so you can write a narrative description.

Read the article "Leafcutter Ants" and answer the questions that follow.

Leafcutter Ants

1. Leafcutter ants are excellent examples of teamwork! That is because they work together to grow their own food. Each ant has a different type of job.

2. Leafcutter ants eat fungus. They grow this fungus from leaves that decay in the forest. In order to grow the fungus in their colony, they must first collect leaves.

3. The ants travel single file into the forest and find leaves. They leave a scent from their bodies on the trail. This helps them find their way back. They use their jaws to cut leaves, and then they carry the leaves home. Back at the colony, the leaves are put in nests and chewed up. Then they are left to decay. This helps the fungus grow and gives the ants the food they need.

4. Here is how leafcutter ants work together to survive:

   - **The queen** lays the eggs in the colony. She spends her whole life creating new ants.

   - **Workers** help the queen take care of her eggs. They also collect leaves and help to chew them up.

   - **Soldiers** protect the colony and watch over the ants when they collect the leaves.

5. Leafcutter ants are truly amazing creatures. We can all learn about teamwork by watching them.

GO ON →

Name: _____ Date: _____

1 **Part A:** What is the meaning of the word **creating** as it is used in paragraph 4 of the article?

Ⓐ becoming

Ⓑ taking

Ⓒ believing

Ⓓ making

Part B: Which detail from paragraph 4 helps the reader know what **creating** means?

Ⓐ The queen lives in the colony.

Ⓑ The queen lays eggs.

Ⓒ The workers help the queen.

Ⓓ The soldiers protect the queen.

GO ON →

Grade 3 • **Performance-Based Tasks**

Name: _____ Date: _____

2 Underline **two** key details that help to explain how leafcutter ants get the leaves they need.

> Leafcutter ants are excellent examples of teamwork! That is because they work together to grow their own food. Each ant has a different type of job.
>
> Leafcutter ants eat fungus. They grow this fungus from leaves that decay in the forest. In order to grow the fungus in their colony, they must first collect leaves.
>
> The ants travel single file into the forest and find leaves. They leave a scent from their bodies on the trail. This helps them find their way back. They use their jaws to cut leaves, and then they carry the leaves home. Back at the colony, the leaves are put in nests and chewed up. Then they are left to decay. This helps the fungus grow and gives the ants the food they need.

GO ON →

Name: _____ Date: _____

3 **Part A:** Why do the ants leave a scent on the trail?

- Ⓐ They do not want other ants to find them.
- Ⓑ They want to attract more ants to the colony.
- Ⓒ They do not want to get lost.
- Ⓓ They want to break down the leaves.

Part B: What is the effect of the scent?

- Ⓐ The ants know where the leaves are.
- Ⓑ The ants are able to carry the leaves.
- Ⓒ The ants are able to call other ants for help.
- Ⓓ The ants know how to get home.

GO ON →

Name: _____ Date: _____

4 **Part A:** What activity do both workers and soldiers share?

　Ⓐ They travel outside the colony.

　Ⓑ They fight to protect the colony.

　Ⓒ They chew up leaves in the nest.

　Ⓓ They watch over new eggs.

Part B: Which phrase from the article supports your answer to Part A?

　Ⓐ "In order to grow the fungus in their colony, . . ." (Paragraph 2)

　Ⓑ "She spends her whole life . . ." (Paragraph 4)

　Ⓒ ". . . watch over the ants when they collect the leaves." (Paragraph 4)

　Ⓓ ". . . learn about teamwork by watching them." (Paragraph 5)

GO ON →

Grade 3 • Performance-Based Tasks

Name: _____ Date: _____

5 **Part A:** What is the main idea of the article?

Ⓐ Leafcutter ants have different jobs.

Ⓑ Leafcutter ants work well as a team.

Ⓒ Leafcutter ants use fungus to live.

Ⓓ Leafcutter ants cut a lot of leaves.

Part B: Which sentence from the article **best** supports the main idea?

Ⓐ "That is because they work together to grow their own food." (Paragraph 1)

Ⓑ "They grow this fungus from leaves in the forest that decay." (Paragraph 2)

Ⓒ "This helps the fungus grow and gives the ants the food they need." (Paragraph 3)

Ⓓ "Leafcutter ants are truly amazing creatures." (Paragraph 5)

GO ON →

Grade 3 • **Performance-Based Tasks**

Name: _____ Date: _____

6 Your class is studying different ways that animals work together. You are assigned to describe how leafcutter ants grow their own food.

Use the article "Leafcutter Ants" to write a narrative description that tells what the ants do from start to finish. To create a well-written narrative:

- Use details from the article to support your description of how leafcutter ants grow their own food. The details may be stated in the article, or they may be inferences based on text evidence.
- Organize the narrative to make important connections between what the ants do and the details you include.
- Make sure readers understand how the ants work together to get the job done.

Use the space below to plan your writing. Write your narrative on a separate sheet of paper.

Grade 3 • **Performance-Based Tasks**

Literary Analysis 1

Today you will read a folktale titled "The Laughing Magpie" that takes place in Sweden, a country in northern Europe. You will also read another folktale titled "The Lazy Farmer" that takes place in China, a country in Asia. As you read, consider the lesson that each folktale teaches. You will be asked to write about the lesson of each tale at the end of the task.

Read the folktale "The Laughing Magpie" and answer the questions that follow.

The Laughing Magpie
adapted from a Swedish folktale

1   There was once a boy named Rolf who lived in the forest with his family. Rolf had six brothers and six sisters. His home was very small for such a large family. It had just one room for everyone.

2   One day, Rolf thought about his home as he walked through the forest. He wished more than anything that his family had a large house to live in. Suddenly, he saw a magpie laughing at him from a tree above.

3   "Why do you laugh, little bird?" asked Rolf. "Can you not see that I am sad?"

4   To his surprise, the magpie answered. "I laugh because you would rather be sad than fix your own problem."

5   "You know nothing about my problem," replied Rolf angrily. "Now please go away!"

6   Rolf waved his arms at the bird, but it did not move.

7   "I can help you," said the magpie. "I will grant you one wish, but first you must complete a task for me." The magpie looked at its feet. "My claws are very dirty. Get me a tool so that I may clean them."

GO ON →

Grade 3 • Performance-Based Tasks

8   Rolf did not know if he should trust the bird, but how many magpies were able to talk? He returned home to fetch a basket. Then he began to pick berries in the forest. Once he had filled the basket, he brought it to town and sold the fruit. He made enough money to buy a sharp tool, which he brought back to the bird.

9   But the magpie had changed its mind. Instead, it desired a wooden bird shaped in its own image. Rolf grumbled under his breath, but he found some wood and used his new tool to carve a bird in the shape of the magpie. It was a fine piece of art. In fact, the magpie liked it so much that it wanted one hundred of those birds before it would grant Rolf's wish.

10   Rolf sighed. He collected more wood and set about the task of carving one hundred magpies. Weeks later, he returned to the magpie with a cart full of wooden birds. "I have done what you asked. Now you must grant my wish."

11   The magpie looked down at Rolf and laughed. "I have changed my mind. After all, where would I put all of those birds?"

12   Rolf became very cross, indeed. "That is not fair! I have fulfilled my part of the deal; now you must fulfill yours. I wish to have a large home for my family!"

13   The magpie continued to laugh. "Silly boy, don't you see that everything you need is right before your eyes?"

14   Rolf looked down and realized the magpie was right. He, too, began to laugh as he turned toward town. The boy sold his hundred wooden birds and made enough money to buy a beautiful large house.

GO ON →

Name: _____ Date: _____

1 **Part A:** What is the meaning of the phrase **under his breath** as it is used in paragraph 9?

Ⓐ very quietly
Ⓑ while speaking
Ⓒ by accident
Ⓓ in a joking way

Part B: Which phrase from paragraph 9 helps the reader understand the meaning of **under his breath**?

Ⓐ "... had changed its mind."
Ⓑ "Rolf grumbled ..."
Ⓒ "... found some wood ..."
Ⓓ "It was a fine piece ..."

GO ON →

18 Grade 3 • **Performance-Based Tasks**

Name: _____ Date: _____

2 Tell what happens in "The Laughing Magpie." Select the **three** most important details from the sentences below. Write them in the correct order in the graphic organizer.

> The magpie offers to help Rolf.
>
> Rolf tries to chase the magpie away.
>
> Rolf sells the wooden magpies to buy a house.
>
> Rolf carves one hundred wooden magpies.
>
> The magpie tells Rolf that he is a silly boy.

1 _____

↓

2 _____

↓

3 _____

GO ON →

Grade 3 • Performance-Based Tasks   19

Name: _____ Date: _____

3 **Part A:** How does the magpie help Rolf?

Ⓐ by giving Rolf a larger home

Ⓑ by making Rolf angry instead of sad

Ⓒ by showing Rolf how to solve his problem

Ⓓ by helping Rolf forget about his problem

Part B: Select **two** paragraphs that show the magpie is wiser than Rolf.

Ⓐ paragraph 1

Ⓑ paragraph 4

Ⓒ paragraph 5

Ⓓ paragraph 6

Ⓔ paragraph 10

Ⓕ paragraph 13

GO ON →

Read the folktale "The Lazy Farmer" and answer the questions that follow.

The Lazy Farmer
adapted from a Chinese folktale

1   There was once a very lazy farmer. Every morning he worked in his **rice paddies**[1] for only a short time. Then, he took a nap and dreamed of a big home and fancy clothes.

2   One day while the farmer was napping under a tree, he heard a loud *thump*. Opening his eyes, he was shocked to find a rabbit had collided with the tree.

3   He smiled at his good luck and took the rabbit home to cook it for dinner. The next day, he sold the rabbit fur at the market for an excellent price.

4   When the farmer returned to his fields, he decided to take a nap without working. After all, another rabbit might run into the tree. If this happened every day, the farmer would never have to work again! So he took a lovely nap, but when he awoke, there was no rabbit waiting for him.

5   Day after day, the farmer napped and waited for a rabbit instead of doing any work. As a result, his rice paddies became overgrown with weeds. The lazy farmer had no food or money. Too late, he realized that he should have worked to get the things he dreamed of having.

---
rice paddies[1]—land used to grow rice

GO ON →

Grade 3 • Performance-Based Tasks

Name: _____ Date: _____

4 **Part A:** What is the meaning of the word **collided** in paragraph 2?

- Ⓐ hid
- Ⓑ ran
- Ⓒ crashed
- Ⓓ escaped

Part B: Select **two** phrases from the folktale that help to explain the meaning of **collided**.

- Ⓐ "... a very lazy farmer." (Paragraph 1)
- Ⓑ "... only a short time." (Paragraph 1)
- Ⓒ "... took a nap..." (Paragraph 1)
- Ⓓ "... heard a loud *thump*." (Paragraph 2)
- Ⓔ "... with the tree." (Paragraph 2)
- Ⓕ "... for an excellent price." (Paragraph 3)

GO ON →

Grade 3 • Performance-Based Tasks

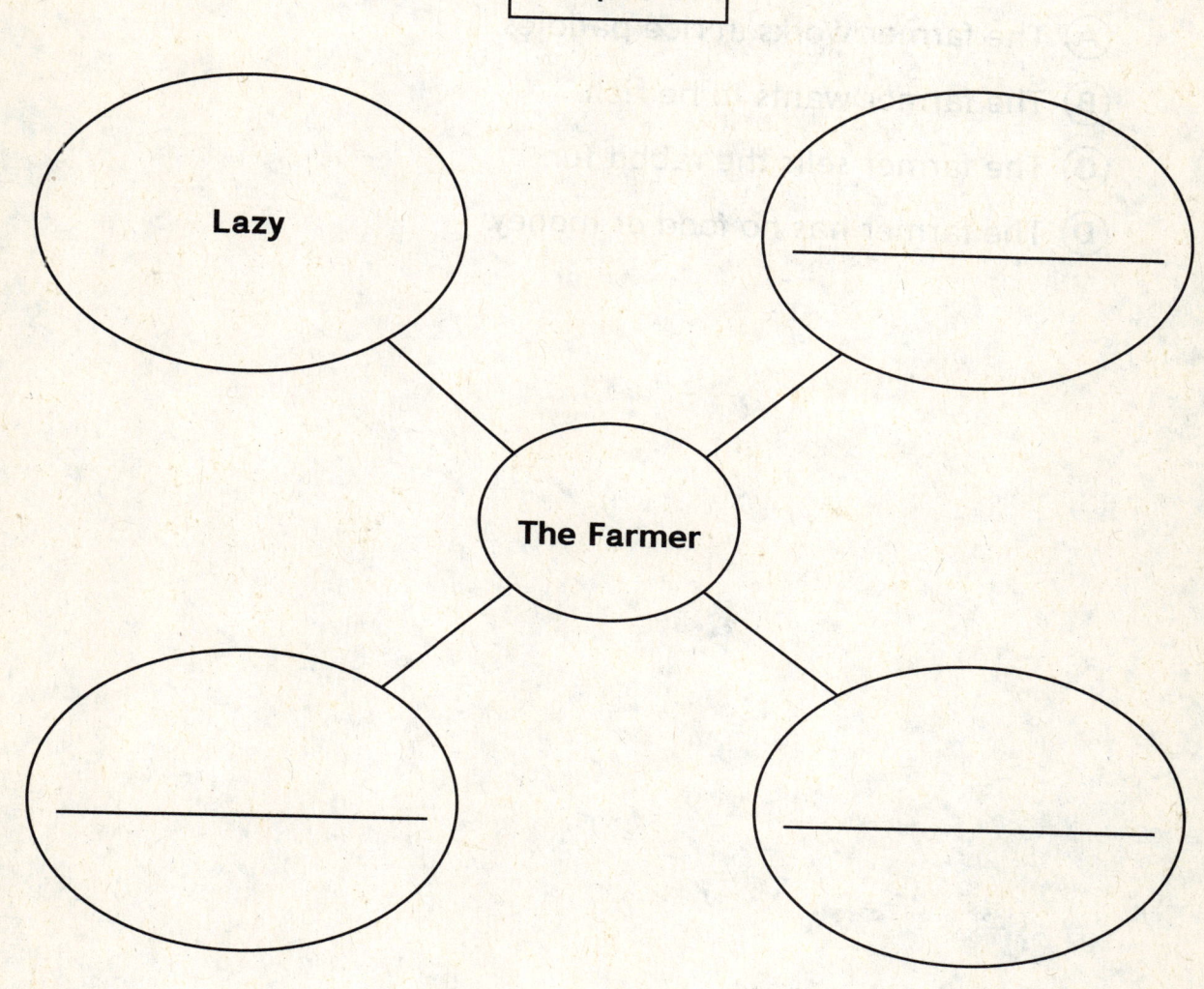

Name: _____ Date: _____

5 Select **three** words from the box below that describe the farmer in the folktale. Write one word on the line in each oval of the graphic organizer.

> Scared
> Foolish
> Lucky
> Careful
> Surprised

(Lazy)

(The Farmer)

GO ON →

Grade 3 • Performance-Based Tasks

Name: _____ Date: _____

6 **Part A:** What is a central message of the folktale?

Ⓐ The easiest way is not always the best way.

Ⓑ Different people have different dreams.

Ⓒ Some people are luckier than others.

Ⓓ Keep trying if at first you do not succeed.

Part B: Which detail from the folktale supports this message?

Ⓐ The farmer works in rice paddies.

Ⓑ The farmer wants to be rich.

Ⓒ The farmer sells the rabbit fur.

Ⓓ The farmer has no food or money.

GO ON →

Name: _____ Date: _____

7 In both "The Laughing Magpie" and "The Lazy Farmer," the main characters learn a lesson about hard work. Write an essay that explains the lesson they learn. Describe how Rolf and the farmer each learn this lesson. In your essay, be sure to:

- Use important details from both folktales to explain the main lesson and tell how the characters learn in it. The details may be stated in the stories or they may be inferences based on text evidence.
- Organize the essay to make connections between events in each folktale.

Use the space below to plan your writing. Write your essay on a separate sheet of paper.

Grade 3 • **Performance-Based Tasks**

Literary Analysis 2

Today you will read a myth titled "Arachne" about a woman who thinks she is a better weaver than the goddess Athena. You will also read a myth titled "Pandora" about a woman who is too curious for her own good. As you read, think about the characters in each myth. You will be asked to write about them at the end of the task.

Read the myth "Arachne" and answer the questions that follow.

Arachne
adapted by Flora J. Cooke

1   Arachne (uh-RAK-nee) was a beautiful maiden and the most wonderful weaver that ever lived. Her father was famed throughout the land for his great skill in coloring.

2   He dyed Arachne's wools in all the colors of the rainbow. People came from miles around to see and admire her work. They all agreed that Queen Athena must have been her teacher. Arachne proudly said that she had never been taught to weave. She said that she would be glad to weave with Athena to see which had the greater skill. **In vain**[1] her father told her that perhaps Athena, unseen, guided her hand.

3   Arachne would not listen and would thank no one for her gift, believing only in herself. One day as she was boasting of her skill an old woman came to her. She kindly advised her to accept her rare gift humbly.

4   "Be thankful that you are so fortunate, Arachne," said she. "You may give great happiness to others by your beautiful work. Queen Athena longs to help you. But I warn you. She can do no more for you until you grow unselfish and kind."

5   Arachne scorned this advice and said again that nothing would please her so much as to weave with Athena.

---
in vain[1]—without success

GO ON →

6   "If I fail," she said, "I will gladly take the punishment, but Athena is afraid to weave with me."

7   Then the old woman threw aside her cloak and said, "Athena is here. Come, foolish girl, you shall try your skill with hers."

8   Both went quickly to work and for hours their **shuttles**[2] flew swiftly in and out.

9   Athena, as usual, used the sky for her loom and in it she wove a picture too beautiful to describe.

10   If you wish to know more about it, look at the western sky when the sun is setting.

11   Arachne's work, though her colors were in harmony and her weaving wonderfully fine, was full of spite and selfishness.

12   When the work was finished Arachne lifted her eyes to Athena's work. Instantly she knew that she had failed. . . .

13   Athena saw her and said in pity, "No, . . . live and do the work for which you are best fitted. You shall be the mother of a great race . . . . You and your children shall be among the greatest spinners and weavers on earth."

14   As she spoke, Arachne became smaller and smaller until she was scarcely larger than a fly.

15   From that day to this, Arachne and her family have been faithful spinners, but they do their work so quietly and in such dark places, that very few people know what marvelous weavers they are.

---
shuttles[2]—tools used in weaving

GO ON →

Name: _____ Date: _____

1 **Part A:** What does the word **fortunate** mean as it is used in paragraph 4?

- Ⓐ helpful
- Ⓑ lucky
- Ⓒ careful
- Ⓓ tricky

Part B: Which word in paragraph 4 helps you know what **fortunate** means?

- Ⓐ thankful
- Ⓑ work
- Ⓒ warn
- Ⓓ unselfish

GO ON →

Grade 3 • Performance-Based Tasks

Name: _____ Date: _____

2 How are Arachne and Athena similar and how are they different? Write the character traits in the boxes of the chart. Write one word in each box.

Character Traits
---
skilled   wise   proud

Arachne	Both	Athena

GO ON →

Grade 3 • Performance-Based Tasks

Name: _____ Date: _____

3 **Part A:** What does the picture help to show about the myth?

(A) Athena turns Arachne into a spider.

(B) Athena's weaving looks like a spider web.

(C) A spider watches the weaving contest.

(D) A spider helps Arachne after she loses.

Part B: Select **two** phrases from the myth that support your answer in Part A.

(A) "Arachne was a beautiful maiden and the most wonderful weaver . . ." (Paragraph 1)

(B) ". . . would please her so much as to weave with Athena." (Paragraph 5)

(C) "Athena, as usual, used the sky for her loom . . ." (Paragraph 9)

(D) ". . . she knew that she had failed . . ." (Paragraph 12)

(E) ". . . smaller and smaller until she was scarcely larger than a fly." (Paragraph 14)

(F) ". . . they do their work so quietly and in such dark places . . ." (Paragraph 15)

GO ON →

Read the myth "Pandora" and answer the questions that follow.

Pandora

1. Once, long ago, Zeus ordered that a woman be made from clay and named Pandora. Zeus then sent Pandora to Earth so that she could marry Epimetheus (ep-i-MEE-thee-us), a good man with a kind heart.

2. Pandora was not only beautiful, but very curious, too. Zeus knew this. He gave Pandora and Epimetheus a small box that was locked and told them not to open it.

3. "Why can't we look inside?" Pandora asked her husband.

4. "It is forbidden," said Epimetheus. "We must obey Zeus."

5. Every day, Pandora stared at the box and wondered. Finally, she couldn't stand it any longer. She just had to open the box! So while her husband was sleeping, Pandora stole the key from him and unlocked the lock.

6. Out of the box flew terrible diseases and sicknesses, feelings of anger and sadness. Pandora shut the box in horror, but it was too late. All of the bad things had already been released to people on Earth. But when Pandora opened the lid again, she saw one tiny thing at the bottom of the box.

7. "My name is Hope," it said in a small but strong voice. "And I will do my best to help."

8. With that, Hope flew away to begin its work.

GO ON →

Name: _____ Date: _____

4 **Part A:** What does the word **forbidden** mean in paragraph 4 of the myth?

Ⓐ not planned

Ⓑ hidden well

Ⓒ not allowed

Ⓓ given away

Part B: Which sentence from the myth helps to show what **forbidden** means?

Ⓐ "Pandora was not only beautiful, but very curious, too." (Paragraph 2)

Ⓑ "'We must obey Zeus.'" (Paragraph 4)

Ⓒ "Every day, Pandora stared at the box and wondered." (Paragraph 5)

Ⓓ "'And I will do my best to help.'" (Paragraph 7)

GO ON →

32   Grade 3 • **Performance-Based Tasks**

Name: _____ Date: _____

5 Sort the details about the myth. Decide which details belong in a summary and which details do not. Write the number that goes with each detail in the correct box in the chart.

Details

1. Zeus gives Pandora and Epimetheus a locked box.

2. Pandora is beautiful.

3. Epimetheus has a kind heart.

4. Zeus tells them not to open the box.

5. The box is very small.

6. Pandora is curious and opens the box.

7. Pandora releases bad things along with hope.

Details to Include in a Summary	Details to Leave Out of a Summary

GO ON →

6 **Part A:** What is the main message of the myth?

Ⓐ Although there may be bad, there is also good.

Ⓑ All rules should always be followed.

Ⓒ You should always be thankful for what you have.

Ⓓ Ask for help while you still have the chance.

Part B: Which detail from the myth supports your answer to Part A?

Ⓐ Epimetheus holds the key to the box.

Ⓑ Anger and sadness are released into the world.

Ⓒ Pandora shuts the box in horror.

Ⓓ Pandora finds Hope at the bottom of the box.

GO ON →

Name: _____ Date: _____

7 Contrast Arachne and Pandora. Write an essay that tells how the two characters are different. Describe what each character does and tell why she acts that way. In your essay, be sure to:

- Use important details from both myths to describe the characters' traits and explain why they act the way they do. The details may be stated in the stories or they may be inferences based on text evidence.
- Organize your essay to show how Arachne and Pandora are different

Use the space below to plan your writing. Write your essay on a separate sheet of paper.

Research Simulation

Today you will research the life of Juliette Gordon Low. She started the Girl Scouts because she felt that girls should learn about their world. You will read the biography, "Juliette Gordon Low: A Guiding Light for Girls." Then you will read the article, "A Chance Meeting," about an important meeting in Juliette's life.

As you read these texts, you will gather information and answer questions about Juliette and the Girl Scouts. This will help you write an essay about the topic.

Read the biography "Juliette Gordon Low: A Guiding Light for Girls" and answer the questions that follow.

Juliette Gordon Low: A Guiding Light for Girls

1   Juliette Gordon Low is famous for founding the Girl Scouts organization more than 100 years ago. Her independent personality and her experiences in life help to explain how this popular group came to be.

2   Juliette was born on October 31, 1860. She grew up in Savannah, Georgia, with five siblings. Juliette was a happy, creative child. She wrote poetry and plays, and she was also very artistic. Juliette loved to draw pictures of the world around her. She had a wonderful sense of humor, as well. Every year on her birthday, Juliette would stand on her head—just to prove she could!

3   Although Juliette loved the arts, she was also an adventurous child. She was happy to be outdoors exploring. She was a good athlete, too. Juliette was a strong swimmer, played tennis, and was the captain on her rowing team.

4   As she grew older, Juliette went away to school in Virginia and then New York. These schools were meant to prepare her to be a "proper" young woman of that time period. But Juliette had other ideas. When she

GO ON →

graduated from school, she traveled in the United States and Europe. She wanted to explore the world!

5   When she was 26 years old, Juliette married an Englishman. Although she moved to England to be with her husband, she still found many reasons to continue traveling and returning to the United States. After all, it was her home.

6   Then in 1911, she met a man who would change her life forever—Sir Robert Baden-Powell. He was the founder of the Boy Scouts. This was an organization that taught boys a variety of outdoor skills that would help them as they grew older. Juliette loved Robert's idea and wanted to start a group for girls in the United States.

7   She returned to America shortly afterwards and began planning the new group. Juliette wanted it to be an organization in which girls could learn to be independent. She did not want them to have to rely on men to do things for them. Instead, she wanted to teach them skills that would help them become strong, confident women. Juliette's group taught traditional home skills for girls for that time period. But it also taught professional skills in the arts, sciences, and even business. This was unheard of at that time.

8   In 1912, Juliette proudly registered her first troop of 18 girls. Her group was called the American Girl Guides. A year later, she changed the name to the Girl Scouts. Juliette's group went on to become one of the most popular girls' clubs in America. Currently, more than 59 million people have been members of it!

1912	1913	1921	1933	1953
Juliette forms the American Girl Guides.	The name of the group changes to the Girl Scouts.	The first Native American Girl Scout troop is formed.	The Girl Scouts start selling their now-famous cookies.	The Girl Scout organization buys Juliette's childhood home.

Name: _____ Date: _____

1 **Part A:** What does the word **founding** mean in paragraph 1?

Ⓐ finding

Ⓑ joining

Ⓒ setting up

Ⓓ talking about

Part B: Which phrase from paragraph 1 helps to explain what **founding** means?

Ⓐ "... more than 100 years ago."

Ⓑ "... how this popular group came to be."

Ⓒ "... independent personality ..."

Ⓓ "... experiences in life ..."

GO ON →

Grade 3 • **Performance-Based Tasks**

Name: _____ Date: _____

2 **Part A:** According to the timeline, when did Native Americans begin to form their own troops?

- Ⓐ 1912
- Ⓑ 1913
- Ⓒ 1921
- Ⓓ 1953

Part B: Which event occurs last in the timeline?

- Ⓐ The American Girl Guides are formed.
- Ⓑ Juliette renames her group the Girl Scouts.
- Ⓒ The Girl Scouts start selling cookies.
- Ⓓ The Girl Scouts buy Juliette's childhood home.

GO ON →

Grade 3 • **Performance-Based Tasks**

Name: _____ Date: _____

3 Select **three** related events in Juliette's life. Write each event in the correct box.

Events:

Juliette meets Sir Robert Baden-Powell.

Juliette travels to different countries.

Juliette goes to school in Virginia.

Juliette starts the American Girl Guides.

Juliette writes poems and plays.

Cause
_____
_____

↓

Effect/Cause
_____
_____

↓

Effect
_____
_____

GO ON →

Name: _____ Date: _____

4 Based on the information in the passage, explain how the Girl Scouts organization has the same beliefs and values as Juliette Gordon Low. Remember to use details from the passage to support your ideas.

Use the space below to plan your writing. Write your final copy on a separate sheet of paper.

GO ON →

Review the article "A Chance Meeting" and answer the questions that follow.

A Chance Meeting

1. "He believes that I might make more of my life . . ." Juliette Gordon Low composed these words in her diary shortly after meeting Sir Robert Baden-Powell. Little did she know at the time how right he was!

2. Juliette was traveling when she happened to meet Robert in 1911. She did not expect to like the war veteran. Juliette had experienced war as a child, and perhaps that had made her feel this way. But when she met Robert, she found that they had a lot in common. They both loved to travel and see the world. They also loved the arts.

3. In particular, Juliette was interested in a group that Robert had started—the Boy Scouts. He had created the group to help teach survival skills to boys in a fun and kid-friendly way. Juliette did not have a real purpose in life at the time, and she felt as if something was missing. She started thinking, "Why couldn't I do something like that for girls?"

4. Perhaps Robert had seen the twinkle in Juliette's eye, for he seemed to know that she would go on to do great things. Juliette created the Girl Scouts in 1913 and never looked back.

GO ON →

Name: _____ Date: _____

5 **Part A:** What is the meaning of the word **composed** in paragraph 1?

Ⓐ wrote
Ⓑ heard
Ⓒ knew
Ⓓ changed

Part B: Which clue from the paragraph supports your answer to Part A?

Ⓐ "'... make more of my life ...'"
Ⓑ "... in her diary ..."
Ⓒ "... shortly after meeting ..."
Ⓓ "... at the time ..."

GO ON →

Grade 3 • **Performance-Based Tasks** 43

Name: _____ Date: _____

6 **Part A:** Why didn't Juliette expect to like Robert?

  Ⓐ He was a traveler.

  Ⓑ He loved the arts.

  Ⓒ He had fought in a war.

  Ⓓ He had not spoken to her yet.

Part B: What happened instead?

  Ⓐ She learned about the Girl Scouts.

  Ⓑ She found they had a lot in common.

  Ⓒ She spoke to Robert about war.

  Ⓓ She helped Robert start the Boy Scouts.

GO ON →

Grade 3 • **Performance-Based Tasks**

Name: _____ Date: _____

7 **Part A:** What is the main idea of the article?

Ⓐ Juliette met Robert when she was traveling.

Ⓑ Juliette and Robert both loved the arts.

Ⓒ Juliette's idea was already taken by Robert.

Ⓓ Juliette's life changed when she met Robert.

Part B: Select **two** sentences from paragraphs 3 and 4 below that support the main idea. Underline the sentences.

> In particular, Juliette was interested in a group that Robert had founded—the Boy Scouts. He had created the group to help teach survival skills to boys in a fun and kid-friendly way. Juliette did not have a real purpose in life at the time, and she felt as if something was missing. She started thinking, "Why couldn't I do something like that for girls?"
>
> Perhaps Robert had seen the twinkle in Juliette's eye, for he seemed to know that she would go on to do great things. Juliette created the Girl Scouts in 1913 and never looked back.

GO ON →

Grade 3 • Performance-Based Tasks

Name: _____ Date: _____

8 You have read two texts about Juliette Gordon Low and the Girl Scouts. Both give information about how the Girl Scouts began. The two texts are:

- "Juliette Gordon Low: A Guiding Light for Girls"
- "A Chance Meeting"

Think about how each author describes Juliette Gordon Low and how she came to form the Girl Scouts.

Write an essay that explains the reasons why Juliette formed the Girl Scouts. Remember to use details from both passages to support your ideas.

Use the space below to plan your writing. Write your essay on a separate sheet of paper.

Narrative 1

Student Directions

Task:

Your class is learning about fables. Your teacher has asked you to write a fable that you make up on your own. Before you write your story, you will read two fables written by the same author. You will also read an informational article that tells about what all fables have in common.

After you have looked at these sources, you will answer some questions about them. Briefly scan the sources and the three questions that follow. Then, go back and read the sources carefully so you will have the information you will need to answer the questions and write an original fable.

In Part 2, you will write an original fable using what you have learned from the two fables and the informational article.

Directions for Part 1

You will now read two fables and one article. You can look at any of the sources as often as you like.

Research Questions:

After looking at the fables and the article, use the rest of the time in Part 1 to answer three questions about them. Your answers to these questions will be scored. Also, your answers will help you think about what you have learned about fables, which should help you write your own fable.

You may look at the fables and the article when you think it would be helpful. You may also look at your notes. Answer the questions in the space provided.

GO ON →

Grade 3 • Performance-Based Tasks

Part 1

Source #1

The Wolf and the Crane
from *The Aesop for Children*

A Wolf had been feasting too greedily, and a bone had stuck crosswise in his throat. He could get it neither up nor down, and of course he could not eat a thing. Naturally that was an awful state of affairs for a greedy Wolf.

So away he hurried to the Crane. He was sure that she, with her long neck and bill, would easily be able to reach the bone and pull it out.

"I will reward you very handsomely," said the Wolf, "if you pull that bone out for me."

The Crane, as you can imagine, was very uneasy about putting her head in a Wolf's throat. But she was grasping in nature, so she did what the Wolf asked her to do.

When the Wolf felt that the bone was gone, he started to walk away.

"But what about my reward!" called the Crane anxiously.

"What!" snarled the Wolf, whirling around. "Haven't you got it? Isn't it enough that I let you take your head out of my mouth without snapping it off?"

Expect no reward for serving the bad.

GO ON →

Source #2

The Wolf, the Kid, and the Goat
adapted from *The Aesop for Children*

Mother Goat was going to market one morning to get food. Her family was not large at all. It consisted of but one little Kid and herself.

"Take good care of the house, my son," she said to the Kid, as she carefully latched the door. "Do not let anyone in, unless he gives you this password: 'Down with the Wolf!'"

Strangely enough, a Wolf was lurking near and heard what the Goat had said. So, as soon as Mother Goat was out of sight, up he trotted to the door and knocked.

"Down with the Wolf," said the Wolf softly.

It was the right password, but the Kid wasn't sure. He peeped through a crack in the door and saw a shadowy figure outside.

"Show me a white paw," the Kid said, "or I won't let you in."

A white paw, of course, is a feature few Wolves can show, and so the Wolf had to go away as hungry as he had come.

"You can never be too sure," said the Kid, when he saw the Wolf making off to the woods.

Two sure things are better than one.

Source #3

What Are Fables?

Fables are short stories that have been passed down through the years. They all share a few common characteristics.

Fables teach a specific lesson, or "moral," about life. Some examples include, "Be careful what you wish for" or "Look before you leap." The moral is often stated in the last sentence of the story. Animal characters are often used to teach the lesson of a fable. The animals act and talk like people do, but they still have their own animal traits. The character of a lion may be proud. The character of a mouse may be timid. Fables may also include plants or other natural elements (such as wind or thunder) that have human traits.

The most famous fables in the world are Aesop's fables. Aesop lived in ancient Greece thousands of years ago. He wrote more than 600 fables during his lifetime.

Fables are interesting to read. They use familiar animals and often funny situations to teach lessons about life. For this reason, they are very popular with children and adults.

Fables include:

- short, often funny, tales
- lessons or morals (often stated at the end of the story)
- animal characters that act and talk like people

GO ON →

Name: _____ Date: _____

Research Questions

1 Based on the two fables, how can the Wolf **best** be described?

Ⓐ helpless

Ⓑ trusting

Ⓒ untruthful

Ⓓ wise

2 Describe the lessons of both fables. How do you know the lesson of each story? Support your answer with details from the informational article and the two fables.

_____
_____
_____
_____
_____
_____

GO ON →

Grade 3 • **Performance-Based Tasks**

Name: _____ Date: _____

3 Identify the features of a fable discussed in the informational article. Which of these features are found in "The Wolf and the Crane" and "The Wolf, the Kid, and the Goat"? Support your answer with details from the informational article and the two fables.

_____
_____
_____
_____
_____

GO ON →

Directions for Part 2

You will now look at the two fables and the article, take notes, and plan, draft, revise, and edit a fable. You may use your notes and go back to the sources. Now read your assignment and the information about how your fable will be scored; then begin your work.

Your assignment:

The two stories you read are examples of fables. Your assignment is to write your own fable that is several paragraphs long. It should includes the characteristics of fables discussed in the article and shown in the stories you read.

Make sure to include dialogue, descriptions, characters, plot, setting, and an ending. Be sure to develop your story completely.

REMEMBER: A well-written fable:

- is a short and often funny tale
- has a lesson or moral about life
- has animals that act like people
- is well-organized and has a beginning, middle, and end
- uses transitions
- uses details from the sources about fables
- develops ideas clearly
- uses clear language
- follows rules of writing (spelling, punctuation, and grammar)

GO ON →

Now begin work on your fable. Manage your time carefully so that you can

1. plan your fable
2. write your fable
3. revise and edit the final draft of your fable

For Part 2, you are being asked to write your own fable that is several paragraphs long. Write your response on a separate sheet of paper. Remember to check your notes and your prewriting and planning as you write. Then revise and edit your fable.

Narrative 2

Student Directions

Task:

Your class is learning about interesting animals. Each student must choose an animal and write a narrative that helps to explain why the animal is interesting. Your assignment is to learn about hedgehogs. You have found two sources about hedgehogs and what makes them interesting.

After you have looked at these sources, you will answer some questions about them. Briefly scan the sources and the three questions that follow. Then, go back and read the sources carefully so you will have the information you will need to answer the questions and write a narrative.

In Part 2, you will write a narrative using information you have read.

Directions for Part 1

You will now look at two sources. You can look at either of the sources as often as you like.

Research Questions:

After looking at the sources, use the rest of the time in Part 1 to answer three questions about them. Your answers to these questions will be scored. Also, your answers will help you think about the information you have read and should help you write your narrative.

You may look at the sources when you think it would be helpful. You may also look at your notes. Answer the questions in the space provided.

GO ON →

Part 1

Source #1

Amazing Hedgehogs

Hedgehogs are amazing little creatures. They are very small, weighing less than five pounds. They are also less than one foot long. Hedgehogs can be found all over the world. In particular, they live in Asia, Africa, and Europe.

These little animals look a lot like porcupines. That is because they have sharp spines on their bodies. The spines help the hedgehog protect itself from other animals, such as birds of prey and wild dogs. The hedgehog rolls itself into a tight ball so that the animal cannot bite it.

Hedgehogs sleep during the day and eat at night. Their name comes from the way they behave. They like to search around under hedges and bushes, looking for food. While they do this, they often grunt like pigs. That is how they got the name "hedgehog."

Hedgehogs are known to eat many types of insects. They also eat mice, small snakes, frogs, and even bird eggs. They eat fruit, roots, and nuts that they find on the ground, as well.

Hedgehogs like cool, dark places. For this reason, they look for holes in the ground. Despite what people think, they do not make these holes themselves. They usually find holes that other animals have already dug. Hedgehogs sleep in these holes for sleeping and raise their young in them. They even hibernate in the holes in the winter. In cold climates, hedgehogs hibernate during the two or three coldest months of the year. Hedgehogs find holes and use leaves and other plants to make a soft bed. Then they curl into a protective ball and take a long winter's nap.

Hedgehogs are interesting creatures because of how they look and the way they act. Even their name has an interesting story behind it. This is why hedgehogs are truly amazing animals!

GO ON →

Source #2

The Hibernating Hedgehog

Hedgehogs are interesting animals. Some types of hedgehogs hibernate for part of the year. *Hibernation* is a type of behavior that is similar to sleeping. It is a lot like a very, very deep sleep.

Why do hedgehogs hibernate?

Hedgehogs hibernate to stay alive. They normally eat insects and small animals during most of the year. But these food sources are not easy to find in the cold winter months. To stay alive, hedgehogs hibernate. Their body systems slow down, and they need a lot less fat to survive. If hedgehogs did not hibernate, they would run out of food and not be able to stay alive.

What happens when hedgehogs hibernate?

When hedgehogs hibernate, their hearts still beat, and they still breathe. But they do not move. Their feet, ears, and skin all feel cold. A hedgehog's heart normally beats 190 times per minute. When it hibernates, its heart beats only 20 times per minute. It takes a breath only once every few minutes. Everything slows down, and its body temperature drops.

How do hedgehogs prepare to hibernate?

Hedgehogs get ready to hibernate by eating a lot! They need a lot of extra fat to make it through the coldest months of the year. Throughout the fall and early winter, they eat as many insects, creatures, fruit, and nuts as they can find.

When they are ready to hibernate, they get very sleepy and they may even shake when they walk. They begin to have trouble staying awake. To get ready, they find nice holes in the ground that are hidden. They create nests made of leaves, grass, and other plants. Then they fall asleep and begin hibernating. In the spring, they wake up feeling thirsty and hungry. They may be weak, but they were able to survive because of their ability to hibernate.

GO ON →

Name: _____ Date: _____

Research Questions

1 Which detail is discussed in both sources?

Ⓐ how the hedgehog got its name

Ⓑ how the hedgehog protects itself from other animals

Ⓒ what the hedgehog feels like after it hibernates

Ⓓ what the hedgehog does when it hibernates

2 Explain what happens when a hedgehog hibernates. Give one detail from each source. Be sure to tell which source you used for each detail.

_____

_____

_____

_____

_____

GO ON →

Grade 3 • Performance-Based Tasks

Name: _____ Date: _____

3 Which source provides better information about how hedgehogs hibernate? Explain your answer by giving two examples from the source.

_____

_____

_____

_____

_____

_____

GO ON →

Grade 3 • **Performance-Based Tasks**

Directions for Part 2

You will now look at your sources, take notes, and plan, draft, revise, and edit your narrative. You may use your notes and go back to the sources. Now read your assignment and the information about how your narrative will be scored; then begin your work.

Your assignment:

Your class is learning about interesting animals. Each student must write about a different animal. Each story must be told from the animal's point of view.

Your assignment is to write a narrative that is several paragraphs long that will help the students in your class know how a hedgehog gets ready to hibernate. You will write the narrative from the point of view of the hedgehog. The narrative will be read by the students in your class, parents, and your teacher.

Make sure to include descriptions and details that show how the hedgehog thinks and what it does as it prepares to hibernate. Include information from the sources using your own words. Be sure to develop your narrative completely.

REMEMBER: A well-written narrative:

- is well-organized and has stays on the topic
- has an introduction and conclusion
- uses transitions
- uses details from the sources to support your topic
- develops ideas clearly
- uses clear language
- follows rules of writing (spelling, punctuation, and grammar

GO ON →

Now begin work on your narrative. Manage your time carefully so that you can

1. plan your narrative
2. write your narrative
3. revise and edit the final draft of your narrative

For Part 2, you are being asked to write a narrative that is several paragraphs long. Write your response on a separate sheet of paper. Remember to check your notes and your prewriting/planning as you write. Then revise and edit your narrative.

STOP

Opinion 1

Student Directions

Task:

Music is important in many schools. However, some schools do not have music programs at all. People have different opinions about how important music is in a student's education.

For this task, you will be writing an opinion article about whether students should learn to play a musical instrument. Before you write your article, you will read three sources. These sources give information about music programs in schools. They also give opinions about how important school music programs are.

After you have read these sources, you will answer some questions about them. Briefly scan the sources and the three questions that follow. Then, go back and read the sources carefully so you will have the information you will need to answer the questions and write an opinion article.

In Part 2, you will write an opinion article using information you have read.

Directions for Part 1

You will now read three sources. You can look back at any of the sources as often as you like.

Research Questions:

After reading the sources, use the rest of the time in Part 1 to answer three questions about them. Your answers to these questions will be scored. Your answers will also help you think about the information and ideas you have read and should help you write your opinion article.

You may look at the sources when you think it would be helpful. You may also look at your notes. Answer the questions in the space provided.

GO ON →

Part 1
Source #1

School Music Programs

Music programs are a part of education in many elementary schools. Often, there is one music teacher who teaches music to every grade. Students may have music class once a week. Schools often have bands or orchestras, too. Students may also learn how to play musical instruments by taking lessons during school time. Then they perform a concert as a group for parents and teachers.

Often, students and their families have a choice about whether they want to play an instrument. Some families may want their children to learn more about music. Playing music has benefits that help students in other subjects in school. So, students are encouraged to play music. Also, kids might feel strongly about wanting to learn to play a certain instrument. They might want to play the flute, for example, or even the tuba.

Other times, families might want their kids to focus more on their schoolwork. Or students might have a lot of activities already. Families do not want them to have too much on their plate. Also, it usually costs money to rent a musical instrument at school. Families must consider this, as well.

Today, school music programs are starting to disappear. Many schools have tight budgets. They have to use their money to pay for things that students need, such as food for lunch and new textbooks. Music teachers and instruments cost money for schools. Some do not think that music is as important as other parts of a student's education.

The future of music programs in schools is still unknown. Only time will tell if schools continue to keep music in our schools or have it become an after-school activity.

GO ON →

Source #2

Every Kid Should Play an Instrument!

In the past, music used to be a big part of every student's education. But today, fewer kids are learning to play musical instruments. This should not be allowed to happen! There are many benefits to playing an instrument. These benefits help kids both in and out of school.

One important reason for kids to play an instrument is that it is good for their brains. Playing music helps kids use and improve memory skills. It gets their brains working in new and important ways. One study of preschoolers shows that kids who took keyboard lessons had more memory skills than kids who did not take lessons. Playing music also helps kids improve their motor skills. These are skills that have to do with their hands and fingers. It makes kids more coordinated. They see the music notes, and they learn to do a certain finger or slide position on their instrument.

In addition, music actually helps students in other parts of their education. Playing an instrument teaches great math and comprehension skills. Kids must learn to count notes and rhythms when they read music. Then they have to understand what to play when they see those notes.

Kids who play instruments are much more organized, too. They learn how to manage their time. Kids need to practice their instruments every week. This teaches them to be more responsible. They also learn to stay with something and improve at it over time. This is an important lesson for kids to learn!

Kids also learn the value of teamwork when they play musical instruments. They must work with other kids who are in the same band or orchestra at school. They have to listen to each other and play music at the same speed to create a song together. This helps to improve listening skills, as well. And kids often make friends while playing in a band or orchestra. Having a common goal as a group builds friendships and improves social skills.

GO ON →

Finally, one of the most important benefits of playing an instrument is that it's fun! Kids who play an instrument feel less stress in their lives. Often, playing an instrument makes them feel happy and good about themselves. For this reason alone, shouldn't every kid be required to play an instrument in school?

Source #3

Let Kids Have a Choice!

School music programs support the idea that all kids should play a musical instrument. They say that it helps kids improve certain skills. It also helps them enjoy school more. But I disagree. Kids should not be forced to play a musical instrument.

First of all, not all kids are the same. They are at different learning levels in school. They also have different responsibilities at home. Not every student will benefit from being taken out of class in the middle of the school day to learn to play music. Many students need to stay in class. They must work on their reading, writing, and math skills. Also, playing an instrument requires a lot of practice at home. A lot of students need to spend more time studying at home. They do not have time to practice their instruments. They might have other responsibilities, too. It is unfair to add to their responsibilities.

Second, some students might have more musical talent than others. Some kids might try very hard to learn to play an instrument. They might work on it day after day. But they might continue to struggle with it. This can be very stressful because they must do something that is too difficult for them. It might have a negative effect. Soon, these kids might begin to dislike music instead of enjoying it. Forcing a child to play an instrument would have the opposite effect of what the school wants.

Third, it costs money to play an instrument. Families must spend money to rent or buy the instrument. It is unfair to require that every kid play an instrument and then to make the family pay for it. Many families are on tight budgets. They may not be able to afford this activity for their children.

GO ON →

Name: _____ Date: _____

3 Which source is more convincing, the second or the third? Explain your answer by giving two details from that source.

_____
_____
_____
_____

GO ON →

Grade 3 • Performance-Based Tasks 69

Directions for Part 2

You will now look at your sources, take notes, and plan, draft, revise, and edit your article. You may use your notes and go back to the sources. Now read your assignment and the information about how your opinion article will be scored; then begin your work.

Your assignment:

Your school is thinking of making every student learn to play a musical instrument. You want to write your opinion about this in the school newspaper.

Your assignment is to write an opinion article that is several paragraphs long for your school newspaper in which you give your opinion about this idea. Your article will be read by the teachers and students in your school.

Make sure to clearly state your opinion and support your opinion with reasons from the sources using your own words. Be sure to develop your ideas clearly.

REMEMBER: A well-written opinion article:

- has a clear opinion
- is well-organized and stays on the topic
- has an introduction and conclusion
- uses transitions
- uses details from the sources to support your opinion
- develops ideas clearly
- uses clear language
- follows rules of writing (spelling, punctuation, and grammar)

GO ON →

Now begin work on your opinion article. Manage your time carefully so that you can

1. plan your article
2. write your article
3. revise and edit the final draft of your article

For Part 2, you are being asked to write an article that is several paragraphs long. Write your response on a separate sheet of paper. Remember to check your notes and your prewriting/planning as you write. Then revise and edit your article.

Opinion 2

Student Directions

Task:

Many people have dogs as pets. They seek out parks that are dog-friendly. Some of these parks allow dogs to run freely off their leashes. Other parks allow dogs, but the dogs must be leashed at all times. What are the pros and cons of each type of park?

For this task, you will be writing an opinion article about whether a new park in your community should allow unleashed dogs. Before you write your article, you will read three sources. These sources give information about dog-friendly parks. They also give opinions about how much freedom dogs should have.

After you have read these sources, you will answer some questions about them. Briefly scan the sources and the three questions that follow. Then, go back and read the sources carefully so you will have the information you need to answer the questions and write an opinion article.

In Part 2, you will write an opinion article using information what you have read.

Directions for Part 1

You will now read three sources. You can look back at any of the sources as often as you like.

Research Questions:

After reading the sources, use the rest of the time in Part 1 to answer three questions about them. Your answers to these questions will be scored. Also, your answers will help you think about the information and ideas you have read, which should help you write your opinion article.

You may look at the sources when you think it would be helpful. You compmay also look at your notes. Answer the questions in the space provided.

GO ON →

Part 1

Source #1

Dog-Friendly Parks

Many towns and cities have parks where people can bring their dogs. These parks are very popular. People in cities do not often have yards or grassy areas to walk their dogs. Dog-friendly parks give dogs a chance to have some fun with their owners.

Some of these parks are "leash-free" zones. That means that people can let their dogs off the leash. The dogs are free to run around and play with other dogs. The area is usually fenced so that dogs cannot run out of the park.

Other parks are "leashed only" zones. Dogs must stay on a leash at all times. Owners are allowed to walk their dogs around the park, but they must stay on a leash and under control. Sometimes these parks are not fenced. They may connect to a parking lot or a street. Often, the dogs must stay on a leash so that they are not in danger from passing cars.

People have different opinions about dog-friendly parks. Some people think these parks should be fenced. They should allow dogs to run off their leashes. Other people think that dog-friendly parks are safer when dogs stay on their leashes. Dogs can still enjoy the park, but they are under the control of their owners. There are pros and cons to both opinions.

GO ON →

Source #2

Let Dogs Run Free!

Dog-friendly parks are popping up in neighborhoods everywhere. They are a great way for people to spend time outdoors with their dogs. Some of these parks require that dogs be kept on a leash. Others allow dogs to be off-leash. This means the dogs can run around and enjoy themselves in the grass and sunshine. This is the best type of dog-friendly park for a few reasons.

First of all, dogs get more exercise when they are not on a leash. They can run around more. They can explore and climb through places that people may not go. Dogs are more likely to play with each other if they are not on a leash. They may take turns jumping on each other and play-wrestling. This is great exercise for dogs. It is much better than just walking on a leash.

It is also more fun! Being off the leash gives a dog a sense of freedom. It can do what it wants when it wants. This is great for a dog that is stuck inside all day. It makes the outside time much more interesting for a dog.

Letting a dog off its leash helps people, too. People are at different exercise levels than their dogs. Often, they can walk only short distances. Their dogs might still want to explore. If people let their dogs off their leashes, they can sit and relax. The dogs can continue to play until they get tired. Meanwhile, people can sit and talk to each other. They can enjoy themselves, too!

Another benefit is that these "off-leash" parks are usually fenced. Having a fenced park is a lot safer for dogs. It is also safer for kids if they are in the park. They will not get hurt by cars or get lost. Even though the dogs are loose, they cannot get away. If a person were in a "leashed" park, there might not be a fence. What if a dog got loose? It could be in danger.

GO ON →

Dog-friendly parks are great whether they require dogs to be leashed or not. But there are definitely benefits when the park allows dogs off-leash. Dogs get more exercise. They get to enjoy themselves and use up some energy. People have a lot of fun, too. And these parks are safer because they are fenced. For all of these reasons, off-leash parks are the best!

Source #3

Keep Dogs on a Leash!

Dog-friendly parks exist in many different communities. They vary in size and shape. They also have different rules for the people who go there with their dogs. Some parks let dogs run around freely. This can be dangerous and scary for many who come to the park. Other parks require that dogs be leashed at all times. These parks are much better for the community as a whole.

Picture walking into a dog-friendly park and being jumped on by a pack of dogs. That can be a frightening experience for someone who does not know a lot about dogs. When dogs are allowed to run free, they often get into trouble. They become overexcited. Sometimes that excitement can turn into nervous energy. The last thing you want is dogs starting to fight with each other because no one is there to stop them!

Some people say that letting a dog off-leash gives the dog better exercise. This is not true. Walking a dog is an excellent form of exercise for both you and your dog. It is a controlled pace over a length of time. Often, when dogs are let loose, they go and lay down somewhere. This is not exercise at all!

Also, when a dog is let off the leash, it wanders away. It can get hurt or stuck somewhere. The owner may not see it and may not know it is in trouble. The dog also might get lost if the park is big enough. Keeping a dog on the leash is a great way to protect it from getting hurt or lost.

And walking a dog on a leash provides bonding time for owners and their dogs. It becomes something special that the pair can do together. Many dog owners say that they look forward to their walks almost as much as their dogs do!

GO ON →

Keeping your dog on a leash is the responsible thing to do. It keeps your dog safe and by your side. It also helps you share the time with your pet. Finally, it makes the park a safer place for everyone who visits it. Dogs will not be able to get into fights. Kids can play in the park without worrying about loose dogs. Everyone can share the park. They can enjoy all that it has to offer. Isn't that the way dog-friendly parks are meant to be?

GO ON →

Name: _____ Date: _____

Research Questions

1 Which details in the first source support the author's opinion in the second source? Provide two details from the first source.

_____
_____
_____
_____
_____
_____

2 Which reason is used to support both opinions in the second and third source?

Ⓐ People can have a good time .

Ⓑ People get more exercise.

Ⓒ People are less scared.

Ⓓ People are safer.

GO ON →

Name: _____ Date: _____

3 Does the author of the third source do a good job supporting the opinion that dogs should be on a leash? Explain your answer by giving two details from that source.

_____

_____

_____

_____

GO ON →

Grade 3 • Performance-Based Tasks

Directions for Part 2

You will now look at your sources, take notes, and plan, draft, revise, and edit your article. You may use your notes and go back to the sources. Now read your assignment and the information about how your opinion article will be scored; then begin your work.

Your assignment:

Your town is building a new park that will allow dogs. The town is trying to decide whether dogs will be allowed to run off-leash or must stay on their leashes at all times. You want to write your opinion about this in your community newspaper.

Your assignment is to write an opinion article that is several paragraphs long for your community newspaper in which you give your opinion about this idea. Your article will be read by parents and students in your community.

Make sure to clearly state your opinion and support your opinion with reasons from the sources using your own words. Be sure to develop your ideas clearly.

REMEMBER: A well-written opinion article:

- has a clear opinion
- is well-organized and stays on the topic
- has an introduction and conclusion
- uses transitions
- uses details from the sources to support your opinion
- develops ideas clearly
- uses clear language
- follows rules of writing (spelling, punctuation, and grammar)

GO ON →

Now begin work on your opinion article. Manage your time carefully so that you can

1. plan your article
2. write your article
3. revise and edit the final draft of your article

For Part 2, you are being asked to write an article that is several paragraphs long. Write your response on a separate sheet of paper. Remember to check your notes and your prewriting/planning as you write and then revise and edit your article.

Informational

Student Directions

Task:

Your class is creating a magazine about climate and weather. Each student has been assigned to learn about a different type of weather. Your assignment is to learn about thunderstorms. You have found two sources about these types of storms.

After you have looked at these sources, you will answer some questions about them. Briefly scan the sources and the three questions that follow. Then, go back and read the sources carefully to get the information you will need to answer the questions and write an informational article.

In Part 2, you will write an informational article using information you have read.

Directions for Part 1

You will now look at two sources. You can look at either of the sources as often as you like.

Research Questions:

After looking at the sources, use the rest of the time in Part 1 to answer three questions about them. Your answers to these questions will be scored. Your answers will also help you think about the information you have read and should help you write your informational article.

You may look at the sources when you think it would be helpful. You may also look at your notes. Answer the questions in the space provided.

GO ON →

Part 1

Source #1

Lightning and Thunder

Thunderstorms can make us want to curl up in bed and pull the blankets over our heads. First, lightning streaks across the sky. Then, there is usually a loud BOOM of thunder. What causes the lightning and thunder? Why do they happen during rainstorms?

Positive and Negative Charges

Lightning is a form of electricity. It builds up from positive and negative charges in the air. Thunderstorms occur when there are a lot of raindrops in the clouds. Sometimes the raindrops are frozen because the clouds are up so high. The higher the cloud, the colder the air is. These frozen bits of ice move around in the cloud and bump into each other. They create electrical charges that fill the cloud.

Some electrical charges are positive, and some are negative. In a cloud, the positive charges are at the top. The negative charges are at the bottom. They also build up under the cloud all the way down to the ground below. Positive and negative charges are opposites. They attract.

Lightning Strikes!

As the charges build up, they get closer and closer to each other. When they finally touch: ZAP! That's when lightning strikes. Because of the way that positive and negative charges work, there are different types of lightning.

GO ON →

Cloud to Ground Lightning

- Positive charge at top of cloud is attracted to negative charge on ground below
- Lightning streak goes from cloud to the ground

Cloud to Cloud Lightning

- Positive charge at top of one cloud is attracted to negative charge at bottom of another cloud
- Lightning streaks across the sky, not touching the ground

Intra-Cloud Lightning

- Positive charge at top of cloud is attracted to negative charge at bottom of cloud
- Flickering light flashes inside a cloud

Do You Hear Thunder?

Lightning is always followed by thunder. Sometimes you hear it and sometimes you don't. It depends on how far away the lightning is.

When lightning strikes, it creates a hole in the air that it passes through. As the air falls back in to fill the hole, it creates a loud sound wave. That is the thunder you hear after you see lightning. It is the sound of the air refilling the space that the lightning created.

You can find out how far away a thunderstorm is by counting how many seconds are between the lightning you see and the thunder you hear. Divide the total seconds by five. This will tell you how many miles away the storm is.

Lightning and thunder occur during rainstorms because the clouds need to be full of water to build up positive and negative charges. This happens in clouds that are tall and dense. When you see these kinds of clouds, you know a storm is on the way!

GO ON →

Source #2

Storm Spotters

Weather centers use a lot of gadgets to help predict the weather. They use satellites up in space. They also use tools in the sky and on the ground. But one of the most important things that weather centers use is not a gadget at all. It is people!

Storm spotters are people who tell weather centers when they see a storm. These are volunteers who live in the community. They are trained by weather centers to know how to spot a thunderstorm. When they see the warning signs of a storm, they quickly call the weather center. The center then warns the public that a storm is on the way!

Sometimes, storm spotters follow storms, as well. They do this to figure out which way the storm is moving. They drive behind storms at a safe distance. Weather centers tell spotters to stay at least two miles away from the storm.

Without storm spotters, weather centers would not know exactly where a storm is or where it is headed. Storm spotters work with weather centers to make sure that people are ready for any storms that come their way!

Signs of a Thunderstorm

- Dark, thick clouds
- Dark sky
- Cooler air temperature
- Increase in wind

Name: _____ Date: _____

Research Questions

1 Which warning sign of a thunderstorm is described in both sources?

Ⓐ how the air gets cooler

Ⓑ how the clouds look

Ⓒ how the sky gets dark

Ⓓ how the wind starts to blow

2 Explain why a storm spotter would count the seconds between lightning and thunder. Give two reasons, using information from both sources. Be sure to tell which source you used for each reason.

_____

_____

_____

_____

_____

GO ON →

86 Grade 3 • **Performance-Based Tasks**

Name: _____ Date: _____

3 How does it most likely feel to be a storm spotter? Explain your answer by giving two examples from "Storm Spotters."

_____

_____

_____

_____

_____

_____

GO ON →

Grade 3 • Performance-Based Tasks 87

Directions for Part 2

You will now look at your sources, take notes, and plan, draft, revise, and edit your article. You may use your notes and go back to the sources. Now read your assignment and the information about how your informational article will be scored; then begin your work.

Your assignment:

Your class is creating a magazine about climate and weather. Each person has been assigned to write about a type of weather.

Your assignment is to write an informational article that is several paragraphs long . The article will help the students in your class know how thunderstorms form and what happens during a thunderstorm. The article will be read by the students in your class, parents, and your teacher.

Make sure to have a main idea, clearly organize your article, and support your main idea with details from the sources using your own words. Be sure to develop your ideas clearly.

REMEMBER: A well-written informational article:

- has a clear main idea
- is well-organized and stays on the topic
- has an introduction and conclusion
- uses transitions
- uses details from the sources to support your main idea
- develops ideas clearly
- uses clear language
- follows rules of writing (spelling, punctuation, and grammar)

GO ON →

Now begin work on your informational article. Manage your time carefully so that you can

1. plan your article
2. write your article
3. revise and edit the final draft of your article

For Part 2, you are being asked to write an article that is several paragraphs long. Write your response on a separate sheet of paper. Remember to check your notes and your prewriting/planning as you write. Then revise and edit your article.

End-of-Year Assessment

Read "A Little Bit of Help" and answer the questions that follow.

A Little Bit of Help

1. "But it's an ORAL presentation, Dad. I'm not sure you realize what that means."

2. Jada stood in the middle of the living room with her arms outstretched. She had a look of pure horror on her face.

3. Ohhh, it's an oral presentation," said Dad. "Well, in that case, what are you worried about? I haven't met anyone who talks better than you."

4. Mom came into the room chuckling, and Jada realized that they were teasing her.

5. She flopped on the couch between her parents and looked down at her hands. Sure, she loved to talk, but not while her entire class was listening. How would she ever be able to get up in front of them and give a speech?

6. Mom saw her worried look and squeezed her shoulders. "Listen—how about we take it one step at a time? You can do the research first. Then I'll help you organize your notes for the speech."

7. "And I promise to sit right here while you practice giving the speech as many times as you want," added Dad, winking at her.

8. Jada took a deep breath and nodded. She was still nervous, but knowing her parents were there to help made it seem a whole lot better somehow.

GO ON →

1 **Part A:** What is the meaning of the word **oral** as it is used in paragraphs 1 and 3?

Ⓐ said aloud

Ⓑ difficult

Ⓒ well-prepared

Ⓓ unusual

Part B: Which sentence from the story helps the reader understand the meaning of **oral**?

Ⓐ "She had a look of pure horror on her face." (Paragraph 2)

Ⓑ "'I haven't met anyone who talks better than you.'" (Paragraph 3)

Ⓒ "Mom saw her worried look and squeezed her shoulders." (Paragraph 6)

Ⓓ "'Listen—how about we take it one step at a time?'" (Paragraph 6)

GO ON →

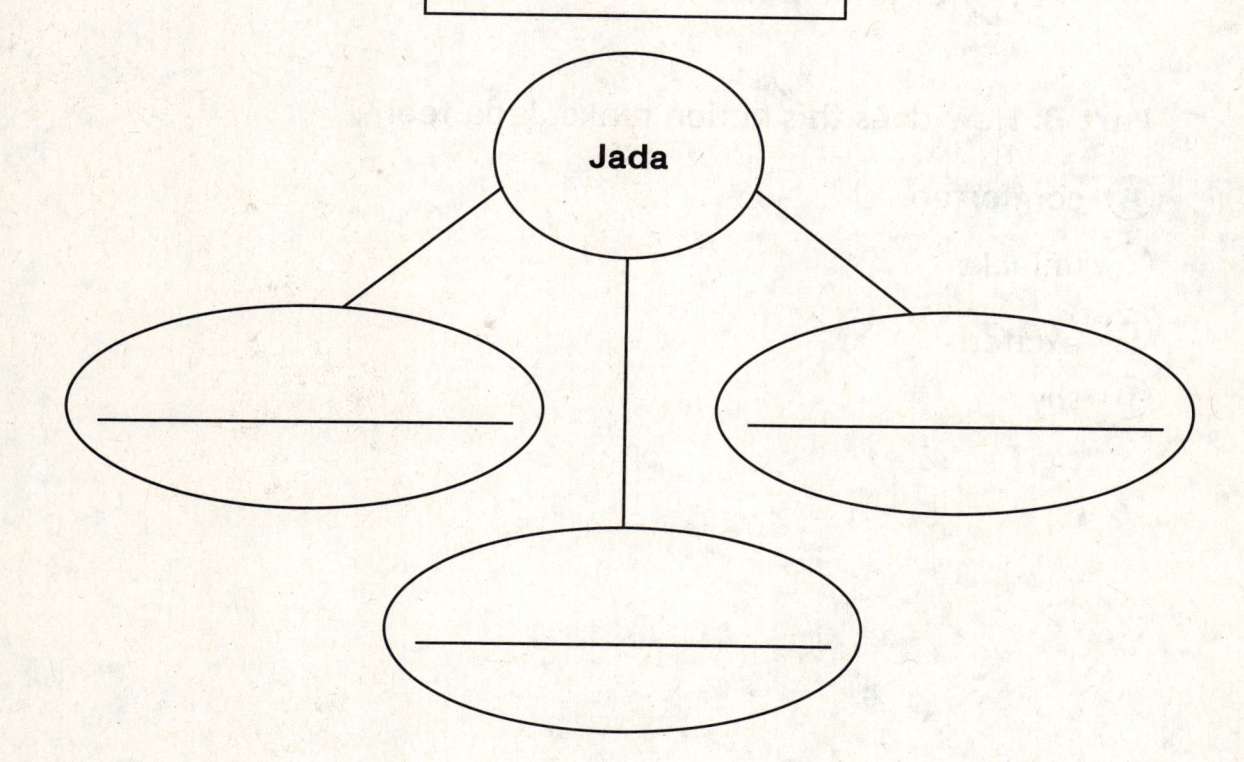

Name: _____ Date: _____

2 Select **three** words that describe how Jada feels at the beginning of the story. Write the words in the character web.

Lonely	Scared
Nervous	Angry
Confused	Upset

Jada

Grade 3 • **End-of-Year Assessment**

GO ON →

Name: _____ Date: _____

3 **Part A:** What do Jada's parents do when they see how Jada feels?

Ⓐ They ask her to do her homework.

Ⓑ They talk about other projects.

Ⓒ They continue to tease her.

Ⓓ They offer to help her.

Part B: How does this action make Jada feel?

Ⓐ comforted

Ⓑ unlucky

Ⓒ excited

Ⓓ shy

GO ON →

Name: _____ Date: _____

4 **Part A:** What happens at the end of the story?

Ⓐ Jada thinks her parents will do most of the work for her.

Ⓑ Jada decides not to think about her oral presentation at all.

Ⓒ Jada is ready to start preparing for her oral presentation.

Ⓓ Jada realizes she has to get most of the work done immediately.

Part B: Reread paragraphs 3 through 7 below. Circle **two** paragraphs that have the biggest effect on the way the story ends.

"Ohhh, it's an oral presentation," said Dad. "Well, in that case, what are you worried about? I haven't met anyone who talks better than you."

Mom came into the room chuckling, and Jada realized that they were teasing her.

She flopped on the couch in between her parents and looked down at her hands. Sure, she loved to talk, but not while her entire class was listening. How would she ever be able to get up in front of them and give a speech?

Mom saw her worried look and squeezed her shoulders. "Listen—how about we take it one step at a time? You can do the research first. Then I'll help you organize your notes for the speech."

"And I promise to sit right here while you practice giving the speech as many times as you want," added Dad, winking at her.

GO ON →

Grade 3 • **End-of-Year Assessment** 95

Name: _____ Date: _____

5 **Part A:** What is the theme of the story?

- Ⓐ Every problem has an easy solution.
- Ⓑ You get more done if you split up tasks.
- Ⓒ Sometimes people will surprise you.
- Ⓓ It helps to have the support of others.

Part B: How is this theme shown?

- Ⓐ through the thoughts of Jada's parents
- Ⓑ through Jada's actions
- Ⓒ through the actions of Jada's parents
- Ⓓ through Jada's words

GO ON →

96   Grade 3 • **End-of-Year Assessment**

Read "Floating Gardens: Aztec Farming" and answer the questions that follow.

Floating Gardens: Aztec Farming

1   The Aztec civilization lived in Mexico from about 1200 until the early 1500s. One of the most interesting things about this civilization was its farming methods.

2   The Aztecs used a very special farming system. Their main city was built on land that was not ideal for farming. It was mostly swamps and marsh land. The Aztecs had to grow their own food to survive. They needed to be creative. So, they built floating gardens called *chinampas*.

3   These gardens were made by laying down mats in shallow water beds. The mats were made of weeds and straw. Then the Aztecs added mud on top of the mats. They planted trees to keep the *chinampas* in place. They also planted enough vegetation to raise the gardens and make them higher than the water level. This resulted in the creation of man-made islands that the Aztecs could farm on.

4   Once the gardens were secure, the Aztecs used them to grow crops, such as corn, squash, beans, and tomatoes. Many of the *chinampas* were also used to grow flowers. These floating gardens made the land both useful and beautiful.

Corn and the Aztecs

- Corn was the main crop for the Aztecs.
- The Aztecs ground the corn into corn meal.
- They used corn meal to make *tortillas*.
- *Tortillas* were a main food eaten with every meal.

GO ON →

Name: _____ Date: _____

6 **Part A:** What is the meaning of **ideal** in paragraph 2?

- Ⓐ important
- Ⓑ perfect
- Ⓒ needed
- Ⓓ steady

Part B: Select **two** words from paragraph 2 that help to explain why the land was not **ideal** for farming.

- Ⓐ special
- Ⓑ system
- Ⓒ main
- Ⓓ swamps
- Ⓔ marsh
- Ⓕ food

GO ON →

98   Grade 3 • End-of-Year Assessment

Name: _____ Date: _____

7 Show how to make a floating garden. Draw a line between each box and the number that puts the sequence of events in the correct order.

1   Add mud and trees to make mats steady.

2   Grow crops such as corn, beans, and squash.

3   Lay mats in shallow water.

4   Add plants to raise garden above water.

GO ON →

Grade 3 • End-of-Year Assessment

Name: _____ Date: _____

8 **Part A:** According to the article, why were the gardens important to the Aztec civilization?

Ⓐ They needed a food source they could count on.

Ⓑ They wanted to make their city nicer to look at.

Ⓒ They had never been able to farm in the past.

Ⓓ They made a lot of money from their system.

Part B: Which sentence in the article **best** supports the answer in Part A?

Ⓐ "The Aztecs used a very special farming system." (Paragraph 2)

Ⓑ "The Aztecs had to grow their own food to survive." (Paragraph 2)

Ⓒ "Many of the *chinampas* were also used to grow flowers." (Paragraph 4)

Ⓓ "These floating gardens made the land both useful and beautiful." (Paragraph 4)

GO ON →

Name: _____ Date: _____

9 **Part A:** What information does the sidebar provide?

    Ⓐ details about the main crop the Aztecs grew

    Ⓑ facts about different foods the Aztecs ate

    Ⓒ details about creating the Aztec floating gardens

    Ⓓ facts about how to grow different Aztec crops

Part B: How does this information relate to floating gardens?

    Ⓐ It helps to show how the gardens looked when crops grew.

    Ⓑ It helps to show where the gardens were built.

    Ⓒ It helps to show why the Aztecs built the gardens.

    Ⓓ It helps to show what the Aztecs thought about the gardens.

GO ON →

Name: _____ Date: _____

10 Complete the chart by writing the main idea and the supporting details in the correct boxes. Use all of the sentences.

> The Aztecs grew crops such as corn, beans, squash, and tomatoes.
>
> The Aztecs used mats made out of weeds and straw.
>
> The Aztecs had a special farming system that helped them grow food.
>
> The Aztecs created man-made islands in the middle of the water.

Main Idea: _____

Detail: _____

Detail: _____

Detail: _____

GO ON →

102 Grade 3 • End-of-Year Assessment

Now you will read two fables that are based on stories from the same author. As you read the fables, pay close attention to the characters, settings, and plots. You will answer questions about both stories.

Read "The Cat and the Mice" and "The Mice Have a Meeting" and answer the questions that follow.

The Cat and the Mice
adapted from Aesop's fable

1   There was once a house in the country that was filled with field mice. The mice lived happily there, stealing scraps of food whenever the master and mistress of the house were not around. They lived a happy, carefree life full of comforts.

2   Well, as luck would have it, a sly cat heard about this house of mice. She was very interested, indeed, for cats quite enjoy snacking on mice.

3   "That's the place for me," said the cat as she licked her lips in anticipation.

4   The cat slipped into the house and set about catching the mice, one by one. She was very happy, but the remaining mice did not like this turn of events one bit.

5   "This is unacceptable!" they cried, and they formed an emergency plan. All of the mice ran to their little holes. They vowed to stay inside until the cat grew tired of waiting and would finally leave.

6   The cat was very clever though, and she understood their plan at once.

7   "How awkward!" she thought to herself. "There is nothing left to do now but coax them out of their holes."

8   And so, after thinking for a moment, the cat decided to approach one of them.

9   "Hello in there," she purred gently into the hole. "Won't you please come out and play?"

GO ON →

10   But the mouse did not budge.

11   The cat tried for hours, and soon she grew very tired of purring and became very hungry. Finally, she realized she needed to try something else if she were ever to get another meal in that house!

12   So the cat climbed up the wall and let herself hang down by her hind legs from a peg. She closed her eyes and remained very still so that the mice would think she was asleep.

13   Soon enough, a timid mouse stuck his head out of a nearby hole. The cat watched it carefully through a tiny slit of an eye.

14   Inch by inch, the mouse came out until it was just out of reach. The cat could barely stand it any longer. Finally, just when she thought she had it, the mouse ran back to its hole.

15   Jumping down from the peg, the cat growled in frustration.

16   "Why won't you come out so that I might eat you?" she asked, too angry to care how ridiculous she sounded.

17   The cat did not expect a reply, but she received one.

18   "You're very clever, Cat, but you may turn yourself into a chunk of cheese if you'd like. You won't catch any of us coming anywhere near you. Your past actions speak much louder than anything you could say or do now."

GO ON →

The Mice Have a Meeting
adapted from Aesop's fable

1   The mice in the country house had a problem: they had a cat that would not go away. They decided that they had to try a different plan. So the mice got together to discuss their options.

2   "We must do something soon or the cat will starve us," whined one of the mice.

3   "If the cat won't go, then we have no choice but to escape to the fields!" announced another one (rather dramatically).

4   "Everyone try to stay calm," said one of the young mice who thought that he was rather good at solving problems. "Here is my solution: We need to get ourselves a small bell and attach it to a ribbon. Then, the only thing left to do is tie it around the cat's neck. That way, we will always be warned when she is coming after us."

5   All the mice thought it was a wonderful idea and agreed that this young mouse was quite clever, indeed, until an older mouse got up to speak.

6   "That is a wonderful plan; it is true, except for one detail."

7   The other mice waited expectantly.

8   "Who is going to put the bell on the cat?"

GO ON →

Name: _____ Date: _____

Answer these questions about "The Cat and the Mice."

⓫ Part A: What does the word **sly** mean in the following sentence from "The Cat and the Mice"?

> "Well, as luck would have it, a sly cat heard about this house of mice."

Ⓐ skinny

Ⓑ pretty

Ⓒ sneaky

Ⓓ lucky

Part B: What does the cat do in the fable to show that it is **sly**?

Ⓐ She enters the house.

Ⓑ She chases after the mice.

Ⓒ She licks her lips.

Ⓓ She tries to trick the mice.

GO ON →

Name: _____ Date: _____

12 **Part A:** What happens when the cat tries to talk to the mice?

Ⓐ They come out of their holes.
Ⓑ They stay where they are safe.
Ⓒ They act like they are asleep.
Ⓓ They run away to find new holes.

Part B: What does the cat do next?

Ⓐ She squeezes into a hole.
Ⓑ She hangs from a peg.
Ⓒ She growls at them.
Ⓓ She chases her tail.

GO ON →

Grade 3 • End-of-Year Assessment

Name: _____ Date: _____

13 **Part A:** How does the cat feel at the end of the story?

- Ⓐ hungry
- Ⓑ pleased
- Ⓒ bored
- Ⓓ forgiving

Part B: What do the mice do to make her feel that way?

- Ⓐ They move into a country house.
- Ⓑ They stop eating the cheese.
- Ⓒ They decide to talk to her.
- Ⓓ They refuse to let her trick them.

14 Circle the sentence from paragraphs 15 through 18 of "The Cat and the Mice" that **best** tells the theme of the fable.

> Jumping down from the peg, the cat growled in frustration.
>
> "Why won't you come out so that I might eat you?" she asked, too angry to care how ridiculous she sounded.
>
> The cat did not expect a reply, but she received one.
>
> "You're very clever, Cat, but you may turn yourself into a chunk of cheese if you'd like. You won't catch any of us coming anywhere near you. Your past actions speak much louder than anything you could say or do now."

GO ON →

Name: _____ Date: _____

Answer these questions about "The Mice Have a Meeting."

15 **Part A:** When does "The Mice Have a Meeting" take place?

- Ⓐ right after the end of "The Cat and the Mice"
- Ⓑ right before the beginning of "The Cat and the Mice"
- Ⓒ in the middle of "The Cat and the Mice"
- Ⓓ long before the beginning of "The Cat and the Mice"

Part B: How does the fable titled "The Cat and the Mice" help the reader understand the events of "The Mice Have a Meeting"?

- Ⓐ It describes why the cat chases the mice.
- Ⓑ It describes why the cat does not have a bell.
- Ⓒ It explains why the mice meet to discuss the cat.
- Ⓓ It explains why the mice must move to the country.

GO ON →

16 **Part A:** How does the older mouse react to the young mouse's solution in "The Mice Have a Meeting"?

- Ⓐ He does not understand it.
- Ⓑ He believes that his idea is better.
- Ⓒ He points out that it has flaws.
- Ⓓ He wants to volunteer to do it.

Part B: Select **two** paragraphs that show what the older mouse thinks of the plan.

- Ⓐ paragraph 3
- Ⓑ paragraph 4
- Ⓒ paragraph 5
- Ⓓ paragraph 6
- Ⓔ paragraph 7
- Ⓕ paragraph 8

GO ON →

Name: _____ Date: _____

17 **Part A:** Which statement **best** describes the theme of "The Mice Have a Meeting"?

Ⓐ Keep your friends close and your enemies closer.

Ⓑ Be prepared to back up your words with actions.

Ⓒ Always learn from your past mistakes.

Ⓓ Do not try to be something you are not.

Part B: Which sentence from the fable **best** helps to express this theme?

Ⓐ "'We must do something soon or the cat will starve us,' whined one of the mice." (Paragraph 2)

Ⓑ "'Everyone try to stay calm,' said one of the young mice who thought that he was rather good at solving problems." (Paragraph 4)

Ⓒ "The other mice waited expectantly." (Paragraph 7)

Ⓓ "'Who is going to put the bell on the cat?'" (Paragraph 8)

GO ON →

Grade 3 • End-of-Year Assessment

Name: _____ Date: _____

Now answer this question about "The Cat and the Mice" and "The Mice Have a Meeting."

18 Show how the two fables are the same and how they are different. Write each story element into the correct box in the chart.

> **Story Elements:**
> Characters
> Plot
> Setting

SAME in Both Fables	DIFFERENT in the Fables
_____	_____
_____	_____

GO ON →

Read "Who's In Charge Here? The Social Order of Chimpanzees" and answer the questions that follow.

Who's In Charge Here?
The Social Order of Chimpanzees

1   Some people think chimpanzees are fun to watch because sometimes they act like people. They are very smart. They also show their emotions. They show happiness and anger and love. Chimps are known to hug and kiss each other and even to hold hands. Sometimes they even act like clowns in front of each other.

2   The best way to try to understand chimpanzees is to look at their **social order**. This is just a fancy way of describing how a group of chimps gets along with each other. Each chimpanzee is ranked in the social order from most important to least important.

One Male Leader

3   A group of chimpanzees is called a **troop**. It is made up of about 10 chimps. Some are males and some are females. There is one male leader of the troop, called the **alpha male**. He's the boss that everyone listens to, but he isn't necessarily a bad guy. In fact, he probably is very well respected by the group. The other chimps would not follow his lead if they did not think he was good at his job.

4   The alpha male is usually very large and strong. He has to be to protect the rest of the troop. But he also needs to rely on the troop to support *him* during conflicts. He cannot fight alone. The other males must stand by his side. They all fall somewhere beneath the leader. Some male chimps are more important than others.

And a Female Leader, Too

5   The females in the group also have their own social order. Their rank is not determined by size or strength, though. They are respected by the others based on their age and their success as mothers. The older a

GO ON →

5 chimp is, the more respect she becomess. Also, if she is a good mother and has babies to care for, the other females look up to her.

Let's Be Friends

6 Chimps within a troop form close relationships with each other. They do this based on their personalities. Certain chimps get along better with other chimps. They may have the same sense of fun, or they might like the same things. This is another way that chimps sometimes seem like people. They make friends based on the same likes and dislikes.

7 Since the troop is small, the chimps treat each other like a family. They usually do not let outsiders in. Suppose another chimpanzee were to try to enter the group. The alpha male probably would scare it away. The other chimps would help him.

8 Chimpanzees work hard to keep their troop healthy and happy. Their social order is a big reason why their they are so successful.

GO ON →

114 Grade 3 • End-of-Year Assessment

Name: _____ Date: _____

19 **Part A:** What does the word **conflicts** mean as it is used in paragraph 4?

Ⓐ times of struggle

Ⓑ feeding times

Ⓒ new births

Ⓓ new places

Part B: Select **one** word in paragraph 4 that gives a clue to the meaning of **conflicts**.

> The alpha male is usually very large and strong. He has to be to protect the rest of the troop. But he also needs to rely on the troop to support *him* during conflicts. He cannot fight alone. The other males must stand by his side. They all fall somewhere beneath the leader. Some male chimps are more important than others.

GO ON →

Name: _____ Date: _____

20 **Part A:** Select **two** qualities that are important to female chimps.

- Ⓐ size
- Ⓑ age
- Ⓒ personality
- Ⓓ success as mother
- Ⓔ ability to hunt
- Ⓕ number of friends

Part B: What are these qualities used to determine?

- Ⓐ whether the chimp can stay in the troop
- Ⓑ the chimp's rank in the social order
- Ⓒ whether the chimp will have babies
- Ⓓ the chimp's overall health

GO ON →

Grade 3 • **End-of-Year Assessment**

Name: _____ Date: _____

21 **Part A:** Which sentence correctly describes an alpha male?

Ⓐ He is the leader of a troop of chimpanzees.

Ⓑ He is at the bottom of a social order.

Ⓒ He is the only male in a troop of chimps.

Ⓓ He is respected based on his age.

Part B: How is this information provided in the article?

Ⓐ captions

Ⓑ key words

Ⓒ a sidebar

Ⓓ a glossary

22 **Part A:** According to the article, why are chimpanzees fun to watch?

Ⓐ They have an alpha male.

Ⓑ They have a social order.

Ⓒ They sometimes act like people.

Ⓓ They sometimes behave like mothers.

Part B: What is one example of this behavior?

Ⓐ Chimps live in troops.

Ⓑ Chimps have ranks.

Ⓒ Chimps help each other.

Ⓓ Chimps hug and kiss.

GO ON ➔

Name: _____ Date: _____

23 **Part A:** Why must the alpha male be respected by the others?

Ⓐ They will not follow him otherwise.

Ⓑ He needs them to help him lead.

Ⓒ They will not survive otherwise.

Ⓓ He needs them to take care of him.

Part B: What probably happens if he is not respected?

Ⓐ He is trained.

Ⓑ He is replaced.

Ⓒ He is angry.

Ⓓ He is ignored.

GO ON →

Name: _____ Date: _____

24 **Part A:** Which information is found under the heading **Let's Be Friends?**

Ⓐ how female chimps figure out social order

Ⓑ why there are only 10 chimps in a troop

Ⓒ how chimps in a troop treat each other

Ⓓ why chimps make friends outside their troop

Part B: Which sentence in this section supports this idea?

Ⓐ "They make friends based on the same likes and dislikes." (Paragraph 6)

Ⓑ "They usually do not let outsiders in." (Paragraph 7)

Ⓒ "Suppose another chimpanzee were to try to enter the group." (Paragraph 7)

Ⓓ "The alpha male probably would scare it away." (Paragraph 8)

GO ON →

Grade 3 • End-of-Year Assessment

Name: _____ Date: _____

25 The statements in the boxes below show **two** cause-and-effect relationships. Based on the order of information provided in the article, write each statement in the correct place in the chart.

Chimps form close relationships.

The alpha male is large and strong.

The alpha male must protect the troop.

Some chimps get along better with other chimps.

---

1. | Cause | Effect |
   | --- | --- |
   | _____ → | _____ |
   | _____ | _____ |
   | _____ | _____ |

2. | Cause | Effect |
   | --- | --- |
   | _____ → | _____ |
   | _____ | _____ |
   | _____ | _____ |

GO ON →

Name: _____ Date: _____

26 **Part A:** What is the main idea of the article?

Ⓐ Chimps have many different kinds of social orders.

Ⓑ Male and female chimps act in very different ways.

Ⓒ There usually is only one leader in a troop of chimps.

Ⓓ Social order in a troop helps chimps live together happily.

Part B: Which sentence in the article **best** states this main idea?

Ⓐ "Each chimpanzee is ranked in the social order from most important to least important." (Paragraph 2)

Ⓑ "Some male chimps are more important than others." (Paragraph 4)

Ⓒ "Also, if she is a good mother and has babies to care for, the other females look up to her." (Paragraph 5)

Ⓓ "Their social order is a big reason why they are so successful." (Paragraph 8)

Narrative Writing 1 Answer Key

Item	Answer	CCSS	Score
1A	A	RL.3.4 , L.3.4a	/2
1B	C	RL.3.4 , L.3.4a	
2A	B	RL.3.1, RL.3.2	/2
2B	C	RL.3.1, RL.3.2	
3A	A	RL.3.1, RL.3.3	/2
3B	C, E	RL.3.1, RL.3.3	
4A	D	RL.3.1, RL.3.3	/2
4B	D	RL.3.1, RL.3.3	
5	**Characters:** Children **Setting:** Outside **Mood:** Worried	RL.3.1, RL.3.7	/2
6	See below	RL.3.1 W.3.3, W.3.4 L.3.1, L.3.2, L.3.3, L.3.6	/2 [R] /7 [W] /4 [L]
Total Score			/23

6 A top response will include a narrative story with the following key points:
- The children address the problem of Snoop hanging off the tail of the kite.
- Bert, Flossie, and Freddie behave in ways similar to how they are described in the passage.
- The story ends in an believable way that is compatible with the earlier details in the passage.

Narrative Writing 2 Answer Key

Item	Answer	CCSS	Score
1A	D	RI.3.4, L.3.4a	/2
1B	B	RI.3.4, L.3.4a	
2	The ants travel single file into the forest and find leaves. They use their jaws to cut leaves, and then they carry the leaves home.	RI.3.1, RI.3.2	/2
3A	C	RI.3.1, RI.3.3	/2
3B	D	RI.3.1, RI.3.3	
4A	A	RI.3.1, RI.3.5	/2
4B	C	RI.3.1, RI.3.5	
5A	B	RI.3.1, RI.3.2	/2
5B	A	RI.3.1, RI.3.2	
6	See below	RI.3.1, RI.3.3 W.3.3, W.3.4, W.3.8 L.3.1, L.3.2, L.3.3, L.3.6	/2 [R] /7 [W] /4 [L]
Total Score			**/23**

6   A top response will include a description of the following key points:

- Worker and soldier ants go out to the forest in single file. They leave a scent trail that will help them return home.
- Worker ants cut and carry leaves back while soldier ants protect them.
- The leaves are brought to the nest in the colony and chewed up. Then they are left to decay so that fungus can grow on them.
- The narrative includes techniques that make the description interesting to read and show the process of how the leafcutter ants work together to make their own food.

Grade 3 • **Performance-Based Tasks Answer Keys**

Literary Analysis 1 Answer Key

Item	Answer	CCSS	Score
1A	A	RL.3.4, L.3.5a	/2
1B	B	RL.3.4, L.3.5a	
2	1 The magpie offers to help Rolf. 2 Rolf carves one hundred wooden magpies. 3 Rolf sells the wooden magpies to buy a house.	RL.3.1, RL.3.2	/2
3A	C	RL.3.1, RL.3.3	/2
3B	B, F	RL.3.1, RL.3.3	
4A	C	RL.3.4, L.3.4a	/2
4B	D, E	RL.3.4, L.3.4a	
5	Foolish Lucky Surprised	RL.3.1, RL.3.3	/2
6A	A	RL.3.1, RL.3.2	/2
6B	D	RL.3.1, RL.3.2	
7	See below	RL.3.1, RL.3.2, W.3.8 L.3.1, L.3.2, L.3.3, L.3.6	/2 [R] /7 [W] /4 [L]
Total Score			/25

7 A top response will include a description of the following key points:

- Both folktales teach the lesson that you will get what you need if you work hard for it.
- In "The Laughing Magpie," Rolf wants a larger house for his family. He gets what he needs by working hard, but he does not know it until the end of the story. Rolf works to buy a carving tool, and then he works to carve wooden birds that he later sells to buy a house for his family.
- In "The Lazy Farmer," the farmer dreams of a big house and fancy clothes, and hopes that more rabbits will come to him while he sleeps so that he does not have to work. He learns at the end of the tale that only hard work will get him the things he wants in life.

Literary Analysis 2 Answer Key

Item	Answer	CCSS	Score
1A	B	RL.3.4, L.3.4a	/2
1B	A	RL.3.4, L.3.4a	
2	**Arachne** – proud **Both** – skilled **Athena** – wise	RL.3.1, RL.3.3	/2
3A	A	RL.3.1, RL.3.7	/2
3B	E, F	RL.3.1, RL.3.7	
4A	C	RL.3.4, L.3.4a	/2
4B	B	RL.3.4, L.3.4a	
5	**Details to Include in a Summary:** 1, 4, 6, 7 **Details to Leave Out of a Summary:** 2, 3, 5	RL.3.1, RL.3.2	/2
6A	A	RL.3.1, RL.3.2	/2
6B	D	RL.3.1, RL.3.2	
7	See below	RL.3.1, RL.3.3 W.3.2, W.3.4, W.3.8 L.3.1, L.3.2, L.3.3, L.3.6	/2 [R] /7 [W] /4 [L]
Total Score			**/25**

7 A top response will include a description of the following key points:

- Arachne is selfish and boastful. She is a proud young woman who thinks she can weave better than even Athena. Her foolish pride puts her in a situation that, when she loses, causes Athena to turn her into a spider.
- Pandora is very curious. Her curiosity outweighs her ability to obey Zeus's orders to not open the box. Because of this character trait, she unexpectedly unleashes many bad things into the world, along with Hope.
- Arachne has several character weaknesses: she is proud, boastful, and selfish, while Pandora's only weakness is her curiosity.

Grade 3 • **Performance-Based Tasks Answer Keys**

Research Simulation Answer Key

Item	Answer	CCSS	Score
1A	C	RI.3.4, L.3.4a	/2
1B	B	RI.3.4, L.3.4a	
2A	C	RI.3.1, RI.3.5	/2
2B	D	RI.3.1, RI.3.5	
3	**Cause:** Juliette travels to different countries. **Effect/Cause:** Juliette meets Sir Robert Baden-Powell. **Effect:** Juliette starts the American Girl Guides.	RI.3.1, RI.3.3	/2
4	See below	RI.3.1, RI.3.2, W.3.2, W.3.4, W.3.7, W.3.8 L.3.1, L.3.2, L.3.3, L.3.6	/2 [R] /7 [W] /4 [L]
5A	A	RI.3.4, L.3.4a	/2
5B	B	RI.3.4, L.3.4a	
6A	C	RI.3.1, RI.3.3	/2
6B	B	RI.3.1, RI.3.3	
7A	D	RI.3.1, RI.3.2	
7B	Underline **two** of the following sentences: She started thinking, "Why couldn't I do something like that for girls?" Perhaps Robert had seen the twinkle in Juliette's eye, for he seemed to know that she would go on to do great things. Juliette created the Girl Scouts in 1913 and never looked back.	RI.3.1, RI.3.2	/2
8	See below	RI.3.1, RI.3.3, RI.3.9 W.3.3, W.3.4, W.3.7, W.3.8 L.3.1, L.3.2, L.3.3, L.3.6	/2 [R] /7 [W] /4 [L]
Total Score			**/38**

4 A top response will include a description of the following key points:

- The Girl Scouts believes in teaching independence and self-reliance to girls.
- Juliette Gordon Low had these same personality traits. She was a world traveler and a creative, adventurous woman.
- The essay will include details from the passage to support points.

8 A top response will include a description of the following key points:

- Juliette Gordon Low had an independent spirit and wanted to pass that along to young girls. She wanted to give girls the opportunity to succeed and be self-reliant.
- Sir Robert Baden-Powell also had a strong influence on Juliette. His ideas for the Boy Scouts and his encouragement for her own plans gave Juliette the confidence she needed to put her plan into action.
- The essay will include details from both passages to support points.

Narrative 1 Answer Key

Item	Answer	Claim, Target	CCSS	DOK	Difficulty	Score
1	C	Claim 1, Target 5	RL.3.9 RI.3.9 W.3.1a, W.3.2d, W.3.3a, W.3.3b, W.3.3c, W.3.3d, W.3.4, W.3.5, W.3.6, W.3.7, W.3.8 L.3.1, L.3.2, L.3.3a, L.3.3b, L.3.6	4	High	/2
2	See below	Claim 4, Target 2				/1
3	See below	Claim 4, Target 4				/2
Narrative	See below	Claim 2, Target 2 Claim 2, Target 8 Claim 2, Target 9				/4 [P/O] /4 [D/E] /2 [C]
Total Score						**/15**

2 Responses should include the following key points:
- "The Wolf and the Crane" teaches that you should not expect any rewards for helping those who are bad.
- "The Wolf, the Kid, and the Goat" teaches that it is wise to be extra cautious and to have two safety measures rather than just one.
- The lessons of both stories are given in italics at the very end of the text.
- The informational article explains that the lesson or moral of a fable is often stated in the last sentence of the story.

3 Responses should include the following key points:
- Features of a fable include:
  » short tales that may be funny
  » a lesson or moral that is stated at the end of the story
  » animals that act like people.
- All of these features are found in both fables.

Narrative A top response includes a multi-paragraph original fable that:
- uses details, dialogue, and description to tell a fable that has a beginning, middle, and end
- establishes setting, characters, and a plot consistent with characteristics of a fable as identified in the source article
- relates ideas to tell a logical sequence of events with a beginning, middle, and end
- expresses ideas clearly using sensory and/or figurative language as appropriate
- has command of conventions, including punctuation, capitalization, usage, grammar, and spelling

[See Narrative Performance Task Scoring Rubric]

Narrative 2 Answer Key

Item	Answer	Claim , Target	CCSS	DOK	Difficulty	Score
1	D	Claim 1, Target 12	RI.3.9 W.3.1a, W.3.1b, W.3.2d, W.3.3a, W.3.3b, W.3.3c, W.3.3d, W.3.4, W.3.5, W.3.8 L.3.1, L.3.2, L.3.3a, L.3.3b, L.3.6	4	High	/1
2	See below	Claim 4, Target 2				/2
3	See below	Claim 4, Target 4				/2
Narrative	See below	Claim 2, Target 2 Claim 2, Target 8 Claim 2, Target 9				/4 [P/O] /4 [D/E] /2 [C]
Total Score						/15

2 Responses might include the following key points:
- When hedgehogs hibernate, their body systems slow down, and they look as if they are in a deep, deep sleep.
- According to "Amazing Hedgehogs," they curl into a protective ball when they begin to hibernate.
- According to "The Hibernating Hedgehog," their heart rate and breathing slows down and their body gets very cold.

3 Responses should include the following key points:
- "The Hibernating Hedgehog" gives better information about how hedgehogs hibernate because (two of the following):
  » The article explains why hedgehogs need to hibernate during the cold winter months (to survive).
  » The article explains what happens to the hedgehog's body when it begins to hibernate.
  » The article gives more details about how the hedgehog prepares for hibernation.
  » The article tells how the hedgehog feels right before and right after it hibernates.

Narrative A top response includes a multi-paragraph narrative that:
- tells how a hedgehog gets ready to hibernate
- is written from the point of view of the hedgehog
- uses details and description to tell a narrative that has an introduction and conclusion
- relates ideas to tell a logical sequence of events
- expresses ideas clearly using sensory and/or figurative language as appropriate
- has command of conventions, including punctuation, capitalization, usage, grammar, and spelling

[See Narrative Performance Task Scoring Rubric]

Opinion 1 Answer Key

Item	Answer	Claim, Target	CCSS	DOK	Difficulty	Score
1	B	Claim 4, Target 2	RI.3.9 W.3.1a, W.3.1b, W.3.1c, W.3.1d, W.3.2d, W.3.3d, W.3.4, W.3.5, W.3.8, W.3.9 L.3.1, L.3.2, L.3.3a, L.3.3b, L.3.6	4	Medium/ High	/1
2	See below	Claim 4, Target 2				/2
3	See below	Claim 4, Target 4				/2
Article	See below	Claim 2, Target 7 Claim 2, Target 8 Claim 2, Target 9				/4 [P/O] /4 [E/E] /2 [C]
Total Score						/15

2 Responses should include the following key points:
- The author believes that students and their families should be able to choose whether the student learns to play a musical instrument.
- Specific supporting reasons include (two of the following):
  » Kids have different learning levels.
  » Kids have different responsibilities at home.
  » Kids have different musical talent.
  » The rental costs may be too high for some families.
  » Kids and families should decide together what is best for them.

3 Responses should include the following key points:
- Student should choose one of the opinion articles as more convincing and describe why. Some examples include:
- Source #1:
  » Playing an instrument teaches kids to take responsibility and organize their time.
  » Playing an instrument is good for kids brains and helps them with motor and memory skills
  » Playing an instrument helps kids learn teamwork when they play with other students.
  » Playing an instrument improves kids' lives by making them feel good about themselves
- Source #2:
  » Playing an instrument can be difficult and frustrating for kids.
  » Playing an instrument can have the opposite effect than what was intended and kids will not like music.

Article A top response includes a multi-paragraph opinion article that:
- clearly gives an opinion about whether every student should be required to learn to play a musical instrument
- uses details from the sources to support the opinion
- is well-organized and stays on the topic
- uses clear language to express ideas clearly
- has command of conventions, including punctuation, capitalization, usage, grammar, and spelling

[See Opinion Performance Task Scoring Rubric]

Opinion 2 Answer Key

Item	Answer	Claim, Target	CCSS	DOK	Difficulty	Score
1	See below	Claim 4, Target 2	RI.3.9 W.3.1a, W.3.1b, W.3.1c, W.3.1d, W.3.2d, W.3.3d, W.3.4, W.3.5, W.3.8, W.3.9 L.3.1, L.3.2, L.3.3a, L.3.3b, L.3.6	4	Medium/High	/2
2	A	Claim 4, Target 2				/1
3	See below	Claim 4, Target 4				/2
Article	See below	Claim 2, Target 7 Claim 2, Target 8 Claim 2, Target 9				/4 [P/O] /4 [E/E] /2 [C]
Total Score						/15

1. Responses should include the following key points:
   - Details from the first source that support the second source include (two of the following):
     » Dog-friendly parks give dogs a chance to have fun with their owners.
     » Dogs can run around and play with other dogs in leash-free zones.
     » The area is fenced so that dogs cannot run out of the park.

3. Responses should include the following key points:
   - Student should state whether the author of the third source supports the opinion well and describe why. Some examples include:
     » Gives reasons why a dog off-leash is dangerous and can get into trouble or hurt
     » Gives reasons why a dog on-leash is safe and has a more enjoyable time with owner

Article A top response includes a multi-paragraph opinion article that:
- clearly gives an opinion about whether a new community dog-friendly park should allow dogs to be off-leash or not
- uses details from the sources to support the opinion
- is well-organized and stays on the topic
- has an introduction and a conclusion
- uses specific language to express ideas clearly
- has command of conventions, including punctuation, capitalization, usage, grammar, and spelling

[See Opinion Performance Task Scoring Rubric]

Informational Answer Key

Item	Answer	Claim , Target	CCSS	DOK	Difficulty	Score
1	B	Claim 4, Target 2	RI.3.9 W.3.1a, W.3.1b, W.3.2a, W.3.2b, W.3.2c, W.3.2d, W.3.3b, W.3.3d, W.3.4, W.3.5, W.3.8 L.3.1, L.3.2, L.3.3a, L.3.3b, L.3.4	4	Medium	/1
2	See below	Claim 4, Target 2				/2
3	See below	Claim 4, Target 4				/2
Article	See below	Claim 2, Target 4 Claim 2, Target 8 Claim 2, Target 9				/4 [P/O] /4 [E/E] /2 [C]
Total Score						/15

2 Responses should include the following key points:
- Lightning is always followed by thunder.
- You can determine how many miles away a storm is by counting the seconds between lightning and thunder and dividing by 5.
- Storm spotters can do this while following a storm.
  » They can then send the information to weather centers.
  » They can also possibly use it to try to get closer to the storm.

3 Responses should include the following key points:
- Student should give an opinion about how it feels to be a storm spotter based on the information provided in the article.
- Details may include:
  » Storm spotters are carefully trained.
  » Storm spotters may follow storms.
  » Storm spotter must be careful not to get too close to a storm.
  » Storm spotters help to keep the public safe.

Article A top response includes a multi-paragraph informational article that:
- clearly explains how thunderstorms form and what happens during a thunderstorm
- uses details from the sources to support the main idea
- has an introduction and a conclusion
- is well-organized and stays on the topic
- uses clear language to express ideas
- has command of conventions, including punctuation, capitalization, usage, grammar, and spelling

[See Informational Performance Task Scoring Rubric]

End-of-Year Assessment Answer Key

Item	Answer	CCSS	Score
1A	A	RL.3.4, L.3.4a	/2
1B	B	RL.3.4, L.3.4a	
2	Nervous Scared Upset	RL.3.1, RL.3.3	/2
3A	D	RL.3.1, RL.3.3	/2
3B	A	RL.3.1, RL.3.3	
4A	C	RL.3.1, RL.3.5	/2
4B	The last two paragraphs should be circled.	RL.3.1, RL.3.5	
5A	D	RL.3.1, RL.3.2	/2
5B	C	RL.3.1, RL.3.2	
6A	B	RI.3.4, L.3.4a	/2
6B	D, E	RI.3.4, L.3.4a	
7	1 Lay mats in shallow water. 2 Add mud and trees to make mats steady. 3 Add plants to raise garden above water. 4 Grow crops such as corn, beans, and squash.	RI.3.1, RI.3.3	/2
8A	A	RI.3.1, RI.3.3	/2
8B	B	RI.3.1, RI.3.3	
9A	A	RI.3.1, RI.3.5	/2
9B	C	RI.3.1, RI.3.5	
10	**Main Idea** The Aztecs had a special farming system that helped them grow food. **Details [in any order]** • The Aztecs grew crops such as corn, beans, squash, and tomatoes. • The Aztecs used mats made out of weeds and straw. • The Aztecs created man-made islands in the middle of the water.	RI.3.1, RI.3.2, RI.3.2	/2
11A	C	RL.3.4, L.3.4a	/2
11B	D	RL.3.4, L.3.4a	
12A	B	RL.3.1, RL.3.2	/2
12B	B	RL.3.1, RL.3.2	
13A	A	RL.3.1, RL.3.3	/2
13B	D	RL.3.1, RL.3.3	
14	"'Your past actions speak much louder than anything you could say or do now.'"	RL.3.1, RL.3.1, RL.3.2, RL.3.2	/2
15A	A	RL.3.1, RL.3.5	/2
15B	C	RL.3.1, RL.3.5	
16A	C	RL.3.1, RL.3.3	/2
16B	D, F	RL.3.1, RL.3.3	
17A	B	RL.3.1, RL.3.2	/2
17B	D	RL.3.1, RL.3.2	
18	**SAME in Both Fables:** Characters, Setting **DIFFERENT in the Fables:** Plot	RL.3.1, RL.3.9, RL.3.9, RL.3.9	/2

End-of-Year Assessment Answer Key

Item	Answer	CCSS	Score
19A	A	RI.3.4, L.3.4a	/2
19B	fight	RI.3.4, L.3.4a	
20A	B, D	RI.3.1, RI.3.2	/2
20B	B	RI.3.1, RI.3.2	
21A	A	RI.3.1, RI.3.5	/2
21B	B	RI.3.1, RI.3.5	
22A	C	RI.3.1, RI.3.3	/2
22B	D	RI.3.1, RI.3.3	
23A	A	RI.3.1, RI.3.3	/2
23B	B	RI.3.1, RI.3.3	
24A	C	RI.3.1, RI.3.5	/2
24B	A	RI.3.1, RI.3.5	
25	**Cause 1:** The alpha male must protect the troop. **Effect 1:** The alpha male is large and strong. **Cause 2:** Some chimps get along better with other chimps. **Effect 2:** Chimps form close relationships.	RI.3.1, RI.3.3	/2
26A	D	RI.3.1, RI.3.2	/2
26B	D	RI.3.1, RI.3.2, RI.3.2	
Total Score			/52

PROSE CONSTRUCTED RESPONSE SCORING RUBRIC

Score	READING Comprehension	WRITING Development of Ideas	WRITING Organization	WRITING Clarity	WRITING Language and Conventions
4	[not applicable]	[not applicable]	[not applicable]	[not applicable]	The response shows strong command of standard English conventions with minor errors that do not impact meaning.
3	[not applicable]	The response addresses the prompt effectively, develops the topic or narrative logically, and is appropriate to the task and audience.	[not applicable]	[not applicable]	The response shows command of standard English conventions with a few errors that may impact meaning.
2	The response uses text evidence to support an accurate analysis of the text and shows a full understanding of the ideas in the text.	The response addresses the prompt, develops the topic or narrative, and is mostly appropriate to the task and audience.	The response is clear and cohesive and has a strong introduction and conclusion.	The response uses language well and includes concrete words, sensory details, transitions, and/or domain-specific vocabulary.	The response shows inconsistent command of standard English conventions with errors that interfere with meaning.
1	The response analyzes the text somewhat accurately and shows a limited understanding of the ideas in the text.	The response minimally addresses the prompt, does not develop the topic or narrative logically, and may not be appropriate to the task and audience.	The response is sometimes unclear and may lack a real introduction and conclusion.	The response lacks clarity, with limited use of details, transitions, and/or domain-specific vocabulary.	The response shows slight command of standard English conventions and has numerous errors that interfere with meaning.
0	The response analyzes the text inaccurately or not at all and shows little to no understanding.	The response does not address the prompt.	The response is unclear and incoherent.	The response lacks details, transitions, and/or domain-specific vocabulary.	The response shows little or no command of standard English conventions and has consistent errors.

NARRATIVE SCORING RUBRIC

Purpose/Organization

4	3	2	1
Organization fully sustained, clear focus: • an effective, unified plot • effectively establishes setting, develops narrator/characters, and maintains point of view • transitions clarify relationships between and among ideas • logical sequence of events • effective opening and closure for audience and purpose	Organization adequately sustained, focus generally maintained: • evident plot, but loose connections • adequately maintains a setting, develops narrator/characters, and/or maintains point of view • adequate use of transitional strategies • adequate sequence of events • adequate opening and closure for audience and purpose	Organization somewhat sustained, may have an uneven focus: • inconsistent plot, flaws evident • unevenly maintains a setting, develops narrator/characters, and/or maintains point of view • uneven use of transitional strategies, little variety • weak or uneven sequence of events • weak opening and closure	Organization may be maintained but may have little or no focus: • little or no discernible plot or may just be a series of events • brief or no attempt to establish a setting, narrator and/or characters, and/or point of view • few or no transitional strategies • little or no organization of an event sequence, extraneous ideas • no opening and/or closure

Development/Elaboration

4	3	2	1
Effective elaboration using details, dialogue, and description: • experiences and events are clearly expressed • effective use of relevant source material • effective use of a variety of narrative techniques • effective use of sensory, concrete, and figurative language	Adequate elaboration using details, dialogue, and description: • experiences and events are adequately expressed • adequate use of source material contributes to the narration • adequate use of a variety of narrative techniques • adequate use of sensory, concrete, and figurative language	Uneven elaboration using partial details, dialogue, and description: • experiences and events are unevenly expressed • weak use of source material that may be vague, abrupt, or imprecise • narrative techniques are uneven and inconsistent • partial or weak use of sensory, concrete, and figurative language	Minimal elaboration using few or no details, dialogue, and description: • experiences and events may be vague, lack clarity, or confusing • little or no use of source material • minimal or incorrect use of narrative techniques • little or no use of sensory, concrete, and figurative language

Conventions

2	1	0
Adequate command of conventions: • adequate use of correct punctuation, capitalization, usage, grammar, and spelling • few errors	Partial command of conventions: • limited use of correct punctuation, capitalization, usage, grammar, and spelling • some patterns of errors	Little or no command of conventions: • infrequent use of correct punctuation, capitalization, usage, grammar, and spelling • systematic patterns of errors

[not applicable]

NOTE: For Purpose/Organization and Development/Elaboration, responses that are unintelligible, in a language other than English, off-topic, copied text, or off-purpose should receive a score of **NS** (no score). However, off-purpose responses should receive a numeric score for Conventions.

OPINION SCORING RUBRIC

Purpose/Organization

4	3	2	1
Clear and effective organizational structure with sustained, consistent, and purposeful focus: • consistent use of a variety of transitions • logical progression of ideas • effective introduction and conclusion • opinion introduced and communicated clearly within the purpose, audience, and task • opposing opinions are clearly addressed (if applicable)	Evident organizational structure with minor flaws; ideas adequately sustained and generally focused: • adequate use of transitions • adequate progression of ideas • adequate introduction and conclusion • opinion is clear and mostly maintained, though loosely • opinion is adequate within the purpose, audience, and task • alternate and opposing opinions are adequately addressed (if applicable)	Inconsistent organizational structure, with evident flaws and somewhat sustained focus: • inconsistent use of transitions • uneven progression of ideas • introduction or conclusion, if present, may be weak • opinion on the issue may be somewhat unclear or unfocused • alternate and opposing opinions may be confusing or not present (if applicable)	Little or no discernible organizational structure with ideas related to the opinion but little or no focus: • few or no transitions • frequent extraneous ideas are evident; may be formulaic • introduction and/or conclusion may be missing • may be very brief or drift • opinion may be confusing • alternate and opposing opinions may not be present (if applicable)

Evidence/Elaboration

4	3	2	1
Convincing support/evidence for the main idea, effective use of sources, facts, and details; precise language: • comprehensive evidence from sources is integrated • relevant, specific references • effective elaborative techniques • appropriate domain-specific vocabulary for purpose, audience	Adequate support/evidence for the main idea with sources, facts, and details; general language: • some evidence from sources is integrated • general, imprecise references • adequate elaboration • generally appropriate domain-specific vocabulary for audience and purpose	Uneven support/evidence for the main idea, partial use of sources, facts, and details; simple language: • evidence from sources is weakly integrated, vague, or imprecise • vague, unclear references • weak or uneven elaboration • use of domain-specific vocabulary is uneven or somewhat ineffective for the audience and purpose	Minimal support/evidence for the main idea with little or no use of sources, facts, and details; vague: • source material evidence is minimal, incorrect, or irrelevant • references absent or incorrect • minimal, if any, elaboration • use of domain-specific vocabulary is limited or ineffective for the audience and purpose

Conventions

[not applicable]	2	1	0
	Adequate command of conventions: • adequate use of correct punctuation, capitalization, usage, grammar, and spelling • few errors	Partial command of conventions: • limited use of correct punctuation, capitalization, usage, grammar, and spelling • some patterns of errors	Little or no command of conventions: • infrequent use of correct punctuation, capitalization, usage, grammar, and spelling • systematic patterns of errors

NOTE: For Purpose/Organization and Evidence/Elaboration, responses that are unintelligible, in a language other than English, off-topic, copied text, or off-purpose should receive a score of NS (no score). However, off-purpose responses should receive a numeric score for Conventions.

Copyright © McGraw-Hill Education

INFORMATIONAL SCORING RUBRIC

Purpose/Organization

4	3	2	1
Clear organizational structure, purposeful focus: • consistent use of a variety of transitions • logical progression of ideas • main idea stated clearly based on purpose, audience, and task	Evident organizational structure, general focus: • adequate, somewhat varied use of transitions • adequate progression of ideas • adequate statement of main idea based on purpose, audience, and task	Inconsistent organizational structure, somewhat focused: • inconsistent use of transitions and/or little variety • uneven progression of ideas; formulaic • main idea may be unclear and/or somewhat unfocused	Little or no organizational structure or focus: • few or no transitions • frequent extraneous ideas; may be formulaic • may lack introduction and/or conclusion • may be very brief, with confusing or ambiguous focus

Evidence/Elaboration

4	3	2	1
Thorough and convincing support for main idea; effective use of sources, facts, and details: • integrates comprehensive evidence from sources • relevant references • effective use of elaboration • domain-specific vocabulary is clearly appropriate for audience and purpose	Adequate support for main idea; uses sources, facts, and details: • some integration of evidence from sources • references may be general • adequate use of some elaboration • domain-specific vocabulary is generally appropriate for audience and purpose	Uneven, cursory support for main idea; uneven or limited use of sources, facts, and details: • weakly integrated, vague, or imprecise evidence from sources • references are vague or absent • weak or uneven elaboration • domain-specific vocabulary is uneven or somewhat ineffective for audience and purpose	Minimal support for main idea; little or no use of sources, facts, and details: • minimal, absent, incorrect, or irrelevant evidence from sources • references are absent or incorrect • minimal, if any, elaboration • domain-specific vocabulary is limited or ineffective for audience and purpose

Conventions

2	1	0
[not applicable]	Adequate command of conventions: • adequate use of correct punctuation, capitalization, usage, grammar, and spelling • few errors	Partial command of conventions: • limited use of correct punctuation, capitalization, usage, grammar, and spelling • some patterns of errors	Little or no command of conventions: • infrequent use of correct punctuation, capitalization, usage, grammar, and spelling • systematic patterns of errors

NOTE: For Purpose/Organization and Evidence/Elaboration, responses that are unintelligible, in a language other than English, off-topic, copied text, or off-purpose should receive a score of **NS** (no score). However, off-purpose responses should receive a numeric score for Conventions.

Grade 3 • **Performance-Based Tasks Scoring Rubrics**